Keep Smilin' Through

MEMORIES OF THE HOME FRONT

1939-45

A compilation of memories from World War II contributed by people who lived in the Chesterfield and N. E. Derbyshire areas during the years 1939 – 45 and others who experienced the war years elsewhere in Britain and later settled here. It gives glimpses of what life was like in cities, towns and villages in wartime over 60 years ago.

These are first hand experiences that record the anxiety and humour of people 'doing their bit' to help the war effort, all affected to a greater or lesser extent by austerity, bombing and evacuation on what was known as the Home Front.

The Editors thank all who have taken up the idea with enthusiasm to send memorabilia and written contributions, and those who have entertained us in conversation. The material has in some cases been edited and extracted from longer texts, but we hope it has been done in a way that maintains the spirit of the originals. We are particularly indebted to David King and the Pro Patria Museum at Renishaw for allowing us, so generously, to draw on photographic material.

The booklet has been compiled under the auspices of the Chesterfield U3A (University of the Third Age) with a grant from the National Lottery, Awards for All Fund.

Editors: Geoffrey Copley, Adrian Marsden-Jones, Jennifer Molloy and Anthony Stroish. Brian Pickering provided the photographic expertise.

Contents

Declaration of war

For the people of Britain, World War II started on the morning of Sunday, September 3 with the announcement by the Prime Minister that the country was at war with Germany. There had been diplomatic activity during the summer of 1939 to avert war, and intense efforts up to the German invasion of Poland on 1 September. Hitler's refusal to respond to a final ultimatum to withdraw made war inevitable. The hopes of the Prime Minister and of millions of people worldwide for 'peace in our time' were extinguished.

Poland ignores Hitler's terms
Time limit that expired on Wednesday
Britain mobilises civil defence
Naval plans completed: Army Reserves called

The Daily Telegraph, Friday, September 1, 1939

The Prime Minister's broadcast

I returned home on Friday, September 1, 1939. "The Prime Minister is to broadcast to the nation at 11.15 a.m." said the announcer on the BBC News that morning. If the King or Prime Minister was going to broadcast, everyone would stop and listen. In those days you did. We gathered in the dining room where the wireless stood. Mr Chamberlain was announced. He spoke. "Poland has been invaded . . . . there has been no reply from the German government to our ultimatum. . . . we are at war with Germany." No one said anything.

Sheila Lacey. Dronfield

Neville Chamberlain

War is announced

I was in church in Baslow with my Mother when the vicar's wife brought in a note for her husband, and from the pulpit he told us we were at war with Germany. I was quite surprised when some grown-ups started to cry. To me it was a new experience and very exciting.

Jean Birkumshaw. Holymoorside

Winston Churchill

Military vehicles

My Father and Mother had taken my Aunt Kitty and I on a family holiday to St Anne's on Sea. I remember coming home in the car, meeting long lines of military vehicles on most of the roads. The news had not been good apparently for a few weeks and Dad remarked that 'he didn't like the look of all this army movement'. Soon after we returned home war was declared.

Frances Showell. Holymoorside

Exciting

At thirteen my first reaction was that being at war was rather exciting, but that impression quickly faded as schoolfellows lost fathers, brothers and homes. Food was rationed and this lasted for several years after the end of the war. An abiding memory from the newsreels at the cinema (no TV of course then) is of refugees fleeing from their homes as the war spread across Europe.

Dinah Evans. Scarborough

Tears

When we got back to school we found many of the adult helpers, teachers and mothers in tears. We gathered that they had been to church where they heard the broadcast of Neville Chamberlain's declaration of war on Germany.

Iris Cannon. Hasland

Is that how it will be?

I was 13 when war was declared. It was Sunday morning and my Mother was making Yorkshire pudding when we heard. I went for a walk across the fields and stood watching the swans on the pond. I thought we are at war and I remembered my uncle who had been wounded in the First War. He had a metal plate in his mouth and I wondered if that was how life was going to be.

Ruby Wilkinson. Beighton

Preparation for war

The worsening political situation in Europe during 1938-39 had given the Government time to make provisions for a possible outbreak of war. Measures to help to protect the population were put into place quickly. The bombing of Britain and the use of gas were an immediate fear. Each homeowner was made responsible for making sure that their premises were blacked out at night, so that lights on the ground could not guide enemy aircraft. Gas masks were issued. Everyone was given an Identity Card and Identity Number. Air raid sirens had been installed and Anderson air raid shelters were supplied to all residents with a garden. Public shelters were built for communal use and everyone decided where they would go in the event of an air raid. The evacuation of children from the big cities started. There followed a period of several months when it appeared that nothing was happening. This became known as the 'phoney war'.

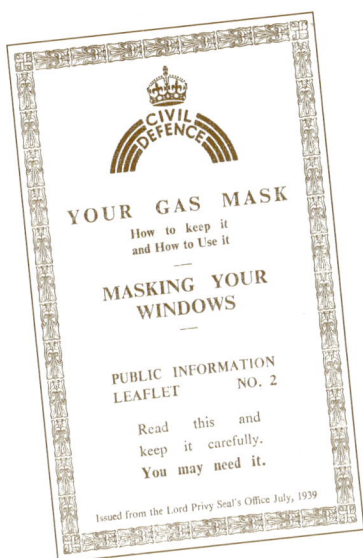

CD Leaflet No. 2

Masking Your Windows

In war one of our great protections against the dangers of air attack after nightfall would be the blackout. On the outbreak of hostilities all external lights and street lighting would be extinguished. Every occupier of rooms, house or flat would be responsible for darkening his own lights.

Civil Defence Leaflet No 2.

Identity Card

Be prepared

Before the war began Air Raid Precautions (ARP) were taught to volunteers. Men and women were enrolled to do various duties as Firemen, Special Police, Air Raid Wardens, First Aid Workers, Heavy Rescue Units etc. in the event of hostilities. The general public were issued with gas masks. Public offices were sandbagged and trenches dug in parks and open spaces. Reservists were recalled to the Colours. I had two uncles who were on reserve and they were back in uniform and with their Regiments. All this happened in August 1939.

Air raid sirens were tested so everyone knew what they sounded like and what to do when they went off. Cinemas, theatres and football matches were all banned, as the gathering of crowds was deemed dangerous. It was illegal to leave the house without your gas mask. Most people carried them in the little cardboard box they were issued in but some had fancy bags specially made, even knitted.

We had all been issued with an Anderson shelter. Those without gardens had a Morrison indoor shelter. There would be no petrol for motoring, so the car had to be jacked up on bricks to preserve the tyres. (It never ran again, after six years it was scrap.)

Peter Rothwell. Walton

'The Siegfried Line'

September 3, 1939 we returned from holiday to try and make blackout curtains or shutters of black paper on wood frames. The British Expeditionary Force had departed for France and morale was high. The most popular song was "We're going to hang out the washing on the Siegfried Line – if the Siegfried Line's still there". Father, Mother, sister and I lived in a modern semi-detached house. We were issued with Identity Cards. Mine was numbered DCKE 95/4. The 4 denoted that I was the fourth oldest. The house had two large bedrooms and one smaller room. As we were two girls and could share a bedroom we had a soldier billeted on us. He was from the Traffic Corps that was stationed in the town. He had been a butler before the war and was the major's batman. He was also a good shot as he was the son of a gamekeeper. While he was with us we had pheasant and rabbit to supplement our rations.

Mollie Lawson. Holymoorside

Balloons

Big balloons appeared above the city. They were fastened to long cables that spread out across the sky, so that if enemy planes came they would crash into the wires. We saw aeroplanes flying over the city. They had two wings one above the other and they chased one another around. Then red smoke would come out of one of the planes and Dad said that it meant that it would have been shot down if it was in a real war. Then someone jumped out of a plane and floated down to earth on a parachute. That was how even if a plane was shot down the pilot could escape and no one would get hurt.

Peter Nightingale. Toronto

Military training

Hunger Hill in the village was chosen for cross-country training of military motorbike riders. It was fairly overgrown with brambles and my two oldest brothers, with other lads, often went out there to enjoy the misadventures and language used by the soldiers when accidents happened. The moorland was also use by paratroops stationed the other side of Chesterfield. Their training appeared to be combat, and a stuffed dummy propped up against a stone wall with many bayonet slashes in it, testified to that. One day a friend and I were pushing our bikes up Belmont Hill when a truckload of troops dressed in new German uniforms passed us. One stood up and gave the Nazi salute while the others laughed. We thought the troops had to be paratroopers heading on to the moors on a mission – at least we hoped so.

Joan Baltare (nee Nightingale). Vancouver

Gas masks, identity cards and disks

I remember how dark it was at night, no street lighting and only the tiniest glimmer on main roads. Vehicles had only slits or deep hoods over the lights. At 8.00 on a dark night the bus arrived to fit everyone with gas masks. The masks were horrible to wear as breathing was an effort and the smell of rubber and chemicals awful. Small children went into a big bag called a 'Mickey Mouse' suit. Everyone had an Identity Card with your name and number. (Your Identity Number later became your National Health Number.) You had to carry a gas mask and a metal disk or bracelet with your name, address and number engraved on it.

Jean Birkumshaw. Holymoorside

Identity number

I can remember my number to this day. You had to know it in case you were mistaken for a German spy.

Harry Husband. Walton

The 'phoney' war Sept 1939 – May 1940

There had been talk of war for months and horror stories of the Germans attacking with bombers immediately war was declared. Stories of bomb attacks in the Spanish Civil War were fresh in everyone's mind. Reports had indicated that bombers always get through. Gas masks had been issued to everyone including babies; windows were splinter proofed with sticky parcel tape criss-crossed; all windows and doors were blacked out; Anderson and Morrison air raid shelters were issued and installed. Schools were closed as most of the pupils had been evacuated to the country.

We listened to Mr Chamberlain's speech on the "wireless" telling us that talks had failed and that "we were now in a state of war with Germany". A quarter of an hour later the sirens went. We hurried to our Anderson shelter at the bottom of the garden, taking our gas masks with us. Four of us Mum, Dad and my nine-year-old sister all expecting to be blown to pieces any moment. Nothing happened, we just sat there waiting and later we heard it was mistaken identity; a friendly fighter had been identified as hostile and set off the alarm. Nothing happened for months. It was a period named the phoney war. Nightly, the BBC News reported, "Offensive patrols were carried out by our forces." Occasionally it was, "Enemy aircraft attacked East Coast areas and were repelled." (The news never revealed the names of towns bombed in case it aided the enemy). But we saw nothing, heard nothing and gradually life resumed some normality. Most people carried lunch in their gas mask case. Cinemas re-opened and football re-started on a regional basis. Teams like Aldershot and Portsmouth from the old Third Division South could turn out a full England/Scotland international side because of the number of Servicemen stationed there.

Peter Rothwell. Walton

Early shortages

After three months we were in the phoney war where apparently nothing was happening. Shops had run out of black cloth and sticky tape to criss-cross windows in the expectation of bombing. Then came food shortages – quite a lot due to stocking up in case of emergency.

Enid Edwards. Chesterfield

Blackout

I was 13 years old when war was declared. We were living on the outskirts of Hull and the most immediate danger was the possibility of air raids. We were issued with gas masks that we had to carry with us (but never had to use). There were no streetlights at night and our houses had to be blacked out with thick curtains so that no lights showed. Putting up the blackout night after night was a chore.

Dinah Evans. Scarborough

Grandma's spotted dick

During the 'phoney war' as it was called in early 1940, the government, worried by the threat of imminent bombing of our cities, urged families to evacuate their children to the countryside. My rather formal grandparents, doing their bit for the war effort, reluctantly took in two young lads in short trousers.

Dinner consisted of a nameless stew followed by 'spotted-dick' as usual rolled in a tea towel, tied either end and boiled in a saucepan. Grandma thought this would be a special treat for the boys. Grandad, serving up, asked the boys, " Who wants an end?"

"No thank you," answered the boys politely. Whereupon Grandad divided the spotted dick down the middle between themselves, leaving the boys speechless.

Stan Sydenham. Holymoorside

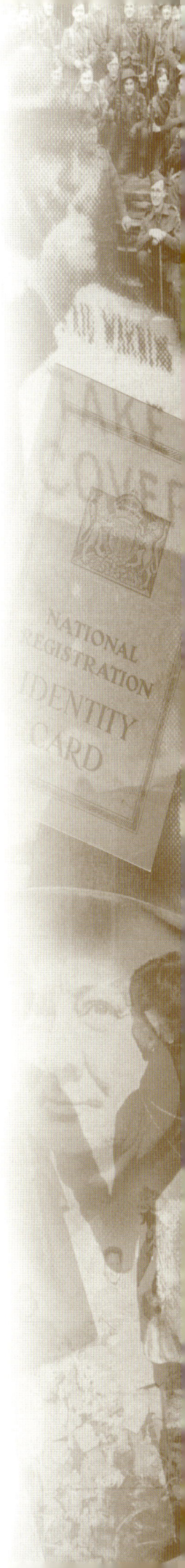

Gas masks

The fear of gas attack on the general population had prompted the handing out of gas masks during the preceding year. They were mass-produced in rubber with a clear visor and a filter on the front. There were special designs for babies. Gas masks were carried in cardboard cartons on string slung over the shoulder. Some people purchased more durable or more elegant containers. Gas masks had to be carried everywhere at all times. When placed over the head, the visor steamed up, they made breathing difficult and they smelt of rubber and disinfectant. Practising to put the mask on became a part of life in the classroom. It was all very serious but humour usually prevailed over any short-term discomfort. Fortunately, they were never needed.

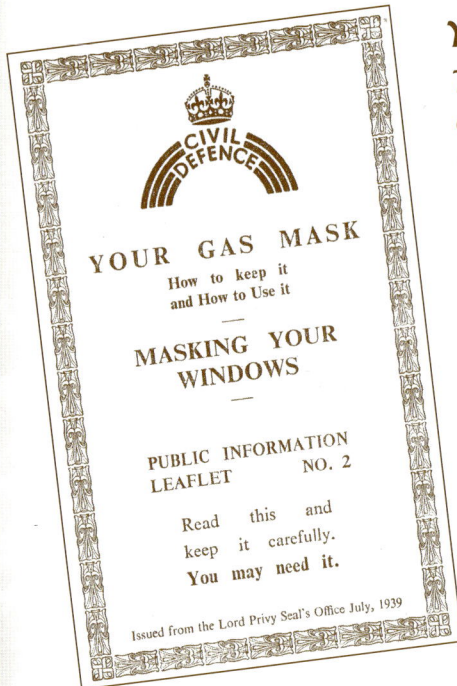

CIVIL DEFENCE

YOUR GAS MASK
How to keep it
and How to Use it
—
MASKING YOUR
WINDOWS
—

PUBLIC INFORMATION
LEAFLET   NO. 2

Read this and
keep it carefully.
You may need it.

Issued from the Lord Privy Seal's Office July, 1939

CD Leaflet No. 2

Your Gas Mask

Take care of your gas mask and your gas mask will take care of you. It is possible that in war your life might depend on your gas mask and the condition in which it has been kept. To put on, hold the mask by each of the side straps with the thumbs underneath and the inside of the window facing you. Then lift the mask to your face, push your chin forwards into it and draw the straps over the top of your head as far as they will go. To remove the mask, insert the thumbs under the buckle at the back of your head and then pull it forward over the top of your head so that the mask is lowered downwards from your face. NEVER TRY TO LIFT THE MASK OFF UPWARDS OR BY PULLING THE CONTAINER OR THE EDGE OF THE RUBBER AT THE CHIN.

Civil Defence leaflet No 2

My gas mask

Everybody who tried one on remembers their gas mask. It has a flexible, black rubber face piece with a plastic window and straps to go over your head. You were threatened with dire consequences if you bent the window. At the front was a metal container filled with a material that would absorb gas. We were told it would be effective against any known war gas and, of course, we believed it. Happily, we never had to use it.

You were told to have it with you at all times, never to hang it up by the straps, as this would pull it out of shape, and always to keep it in the special container that was provided.

Gas mask

You were instructed how to put it on and take it off and we practised regularly at school. It always misted up and became wet inside. You had to dry it each time you used it. To stop the window misting you were told to wet the end of your finger, rup it on a piece of soap, and then rub it on the inside of the window. The same treatment works quite well on my glasses today.

Anon

Gas mask practice

Gas mask practice became a routine in the classroom together with getting under the desk if the air raid warning sounded. The teacher had to carry out a test of the seals by holding a card under the filter at the front of the mask as you tried to hold it there by breathing in. I didn't put the thoughts together at the time but the school caretaker had a hoarse, painful-sounding voice as a result of being gassed in the First World War.

Geoffrey Copley. Holymoorside

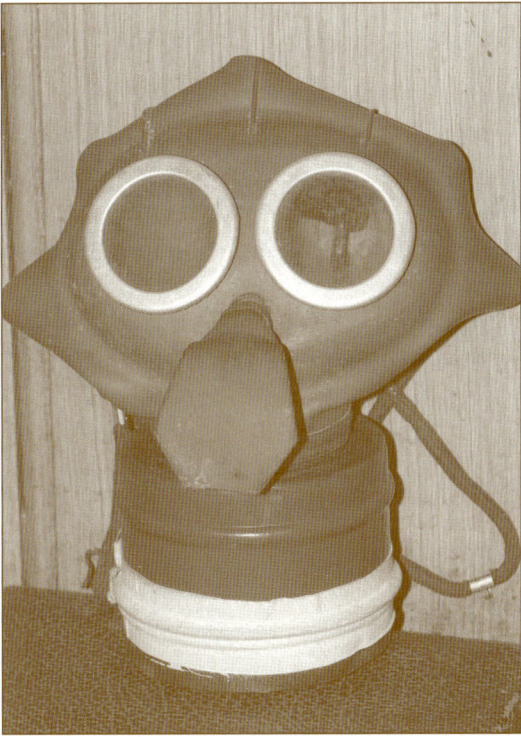

Gas mask for a child

'Was that you Jones?'

Gas masks generally steamed up after a few minutes and I think we were quite frightened with them on. During practice at school, by blowing out vigorously, the rubber flapped on our cheeks making a rude 'raspberry' noise, much to the annoyance of the teachers.

"Was that you Jones making that vulgar noise?"

"No Miss!"

Adrian Marsden-Jones. Holymoorside

Gas masks were awful

Gas masks were awful. We couldn't wear them for more than a few frightening minutes, it felt as if you were suffocating. In the Guides we could get a green 'Bulldog Badge' for war training – learning the smell of gas (like almonds), practising with a warden's wooden rattle to warn of gas and learning how to tape on an extra filter on the bottom of a gas mask. There was a Mickey Mouse gas mask for the young and the baby one had bellows on the side.

Iris Husband. Holymoorside

Bend down by the hedge

At school we were issued with gas masks and had to write our name on the box. We were told to carry it always, never leave it anywhere and hang it by the string on the back of your chair during lessons. We had no air raid shelter at school and we were told that if there was an air raid we should go outside and bend down under the hedge!

Ruby Wilkinson. Beighton

Evacuation

When Hitler attacked Poland on 1 September, plans to evacuate children from the danger of bombing in big cities were put into action. On the first morning, large numbers of children, labelled and carrying their gas masks and clothes, headed for buses and railway stations with their teachers. There was no compulsion, but the fear of bombing was so great that many parents decided that their children should go. Any household with a spare room had to take one or more evacuees. On arrival, there were 'pick-your-evacuee' sessions where hosts picked the ones they liked the look of. For some children evacuation was traumatic and brothers and sisters could be separated, perhaps never to meet again. For others it was the start of a new life. Many retain clear memories of the experience.

Evacuation – why and how?

If we were involved in war, our big cities might be subjected to determined attacks from the air … some bombers would undoubtedly get through. We must see to it that the enemy does not achieve his chief objects – the creation of panic or the crippling dislocation of our civil life. One of the first measures we can take to prevent this is the removal of children from the more dangerous areas.

Civil Defence Leaflet No 3

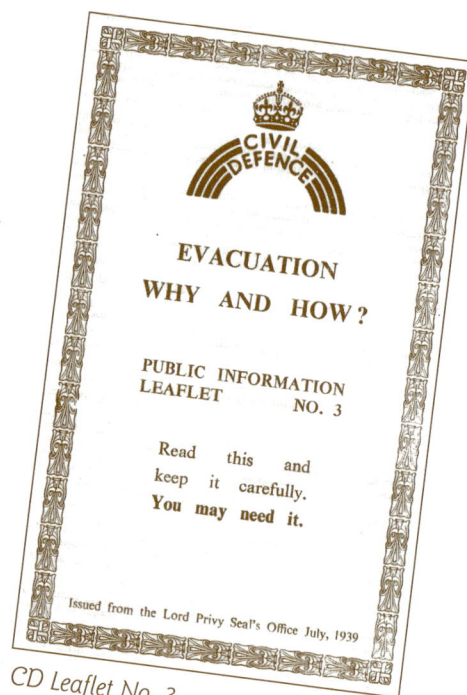

CD Leaflet No. 3

Evacuation to Holymoorside I

Evacuation turned out to have long-term ramifications. In the summer of 1939 the family lived in Ilford. Our parents were very aware of the dangers posed by Germany and its capability to bomb London. The house was close to the railway line and would be a dangerous place when bombing started, so they decided to leave the London area. This turned out to be a wise move because within two years a bomb destroyed the house.

The three children, aged 12, 8 and 6 years old, were evacuated first to Suffolk and taken to the village hall in Debenham. Mother had stipulated that we must be kept together with the eldest, our sister, in charge. Throughout the day people came into the hall and chose the children they would look after. After teatime, we three children were left, as no one wanted three together. So the lady in charge put the three of us into her car and drove us two miles out of the village to a farm. The farmer's wife had said that if there was no other alternative she would take two but no more. She was morally blackmailed into taking all three as the organising lady owned the farm. So we were selected by default.

The farmer already had two children who could do no wrong so the visiting children were blamed for everything. Needless to say, the resident children took full advantage.

There were rules for we visitors set by the farmer and his wife. These are a few of them:

stand to attention when an adult came into the room; specific chores to do each day, for example, one had to clean the toilet and bath, another wash all the pots; we were not allowed to participate in any family activity except meals; immediately after tea we were shut in our room under the supervision of the eldest until bedtime; every Sunday

Evacuees

afternoon, whatever the weather, we were shut out of the house and not allowed in until 6 p.m.

Every day we walked 2 miles to the school in the village and back again at the end of school.

Meanwhile our parents in London were working out the second stage of the move. They had family ties in Derbyshire and this is where they looked for help in their move from London. They found a suitable house to rent in Holymoorside and set about reuniting the family. Petrol was rationed, so it was not possible to get vans to move the contents of the house and these had to be left in London. Relatives and second hand shops provided the furniture for the new house.

Holymoorside was a close community village at that time. Strangers were viewed with suspicion and not easily integrated. We were the first evacuee family in the village. Others followed and perhaps their integration was smoother. The village culture was quite violent with adults often fighting to establish a pecking order or to settle domestic disputes. Yet there was a warmth and caring in the community. In most cases they looked after people who needed help. Anyway we settled and our youngest brother, born in the village during the war, is still resident there.

Peter Nightingale. Toronto

Evacuation to Holymoorside II

We had always been a secure family and a happy one. We lived in a commuter suburb of London but had always been into the countryside at weekends. Consequently the countryside was associated with pleasure.

When the war started my elder sister, younger brother and I were evacuated to a village near Ipswich leaving behind my Mother, Father and four-year-old brother. My Father stayed in London while my Mother and brother moved to my uncle's house in Cromford. The experience of being an evacuee was traumatic. We had been told that we were going for a week's holiday. When the week finished we remained but were not told why for a long time. I had never been in a home where I was not wanted and, as children often do, I knew that I was unwelcome. The experience stopped me communicating with the adults as it was used against me. Everything I said was derided and I was sharply put down.

At the beginning of December we heard that my Father would be coming to take us to a new home for Christmas. So we had a journey to Holymoorside. Gradually I began to regain some of my confidence but then talk began about my Father having to leave home to work for the war and I had nothing but fear when we started school again after Christmas.

There were two main difficulties in the school. One was the local accent. On one occasion I went home and asked what was meant when someone said, "What's thou 'anging tap on for?" It took me a long time to understand what some of the children were saying and my accent marked me as different. I did not feel that I belonged. Fortunately I had been to a good school in London so the school work was no problem.

I was horrified to see children being hit and caned by the teachers. This had not happened in my previous school. There was fighting between the gangs that I found frightening and did not understand. Bullying was accepted and the staff did not control it.

The area in which we had lived in London was not one where you could play in the streets. We had to go to the park. The freedom of the village was wonderful and its beauty thrilled me. We did not have to be watched or protected and this was a great bonus. However, for a long time my feeling was of insecurity, isolation, fear and anxiety. I had great faith in my parents that enabled me gradually to become accustomed to the village and its ways.

F. H. Cross (née Nightingale). Duns Tew

My first evacuation

Late in August it was thought that war was imminent and that the bombing of London would begin as soon as war was declared, so it was essential to move schoolchildren and mothers and babies quickly. I went with my school party and other schools on one of the river pleasure boats, along the Thames and then up the coast to Lowestoft in Suffolk. The boats were specially commissioned for the emergency and later were to be involved in the evacuation of our troops from Dunkirk. Nothing had been planned for our arrival, so for a few days we had to sleep on straw spread on the floor of the school classroom and had food on desks in the playground (lucky for us the sun was shining).

On Sunday, September 5, some local young women took the children to the beach. I remember getting told off because I had taken my gas mask from its cardboard box to use it for collecting shells. I realise now that the prevailing hysteria was caused by the belief that we were all going to be gassed at any moment.

The local population realised that we were there to stay and rapidly made arrangements for us to be sent to neighbouring towns and villages where billets were found. Our party went to Beccles where a pleasant family, with two children, welcomed me to their small terrace house.

However this winter was the time of the 'phoney' war where nothing seemed to be happening in London. People thought it was a false alarm and started to drift home. I went home and stayed for the first few months of 1940.

Iris Cannon. Hasland

Family evacuation

It was Sunday morning, September 3, 1939 when the family were bundled into a friend's car bound for the safer countryside. We could see worried groups of people hanging over garden gates trying to find comfort in their numbers. The radio told us that Mr. Chamberlain had been trying to negotiate a peace deal as a last ditch attempt to avert war but to no avail. When we arrived our family, Dad (a teacher), Mum, brother John (5) and I (13), were told that accommodation had been found for us at the home of a single lady who seemed to be overwhelmed by this mass invasion, particularly a small boy (she had reason to be). After a week Mum announced that she could no longer tolerate the sound of rats traversing the hollow behind our heads at night. John and I thought that Mum was doing her 'drama queen' routine but it had the desired effect and we were placed quite happily with a small family with no rats to Mother's knowledge. Dad had to return to London immediately as teachers were very scarce.

Enid Edwards. Walton

My second evacuation

In the spring of 1940 another official campaign for evacuation started in the belief that raids would start soon. People did not believe the rumours this time and few children were sent away. There was a rapid change of mood when Germany began the invasion of France and it became obvious that London and the South would be a danger zone. We were sent away again but not to the east coast which was now considered as dangerous as London. I went to the small village of Ransbury in Wiltshire. The locals were ready for us this time and were waiting in the playground of the village school. It was like a slave market – people chose the children they liked the look of and took them off. One farmer chose four little girls, including me, to take home to his wife. We were not very happy as no-one took much notice of us and we were left very much to our own devices. It would have been exciting if we had been older. I was the oldest at 10 and at one time tried to organise our escape. We hid behind the hedge when the school bus pulled up outside the farm until the bus driver gave up and drove away. We did not get very far – all signposts had been removed in case of invasion – and I had no idea which was the direction for London. The other three were whining and I was relieved when an amused teacher caught up with us and took us back to the farm. My parents were informed and my Mother arrived. She was not pleased with the state of the farm and found us a more comfortable billet in the village with an elderly couple. Their son was in the army and we were able to have his room. We stayed until August.

Iris Cannon. Hasland

My third evacuation

It was time for me to go to secondary school and my parents had been informed that I had passed the scholarship examination that I had taken earlier in the year and forgotten. I had to join the grammar school they had selected but, as the blitz had started with a vengeance, the school had been evacuated to Ilfracombe and I went back to the seaside again.

I joined a group of girls in a large guest-house but large houses were rapidly commandeered by the army and I was sent to two other billets in the town. At neither were evacuees welcome – householders had to accept evacuees if they had a spare room.

Finally in late 1943 most of the air raids stopped and I was allowed to return home.

This was the end of my evacuation experiences despite the flying bomb raids in 1944. At 14 I was old enough to go to work and to insist that I was not leaving home again.

Iris Cannon. Hasland

Evacuation to Derbyshire

With the continued bombing of Coventry, my brothers and I were evacuated first to Kenilworth and then to Ashford in the Water in Derbyshire. This was the start of four adventurous years. Not for us the sad image of groups of bewildered children, with their string-bound parcel of belongings and gas mask waving a forlorn goodbye. I had the company of my brothers, an idyllic cottage in which to live and the countryside was a new experience for townies that left a significant and lasting impression.

Adrian Marsden-Jones. Holymoorside

Evacuation to Wales

When I was eight I was billeted with my three older brothers in a large house in the Gower in South Wales. We shared it with three "Kindertransport" Jewish boys aged 13 to 15 years. They had been rescued from German persecution in Austria and Czechoslovakia before the war. They had a carefree disposition and led us into situations that in normal times Mum and Dad would not have approved, like building unseaworthy canoes from canvas and bamboo, and taming wild Welsh ponies.

It was their initiative that enabled us to make our own crystal sets from torch batteries, wire, a semiconductor crystal and earphones. These were assembled under the bedclothes with the aerial trailing out of the window. They took great patience to tune by bringing the fine wire (the 'cat's whisker') to just the right point on the crystal.

"Hey! I've got Radio Luxemburg." A muffled shout would be heard from under the bedclothes, whereupon we would all jump on the bed to try to listen and the connection would be lost.

Our favourite programme was ITMA. "Can I do you now, sir?" and "This is Fumff speaking." Most of all we liked to listen to the latest hits "Moonlight Serenade" and Chatanooga Choo Choo" (Glen Miller), "Boogie Woogie Bugle Boy" (the Andrews Sisters) and "Deep in the Heart of Texas" (Bing Crosby).

Adrian Marsden-Jones. Holymoorside

Evacuation to Colne

Along with my sister Ethel, four years older, we attended Lillycroft School in Bradford. We were in morning assembly when our Headmaster informed us that that we were to go home and return to school in one hour as all children were to be evacuated to a place away from Bradford. We returned from school as instructed where we were loaded on to buses with all our belongings, not forgetting the gas mask. We each had a label with our name attached to our coat. We did not know where we were going. Our destination turned out to be Colne in Lancashire. We were instructed to stay on the bus until a home could be found for us. Some of the local people just wanted a girl or a boy, but not both. This is how brothers and sisters came to split up. Ethel and I were the last off but remained together.

We settled in our new home a little nervously but the house and people were nice. We started our new school but saw none of the children who had come with us.

We got homesick, as we had never been away for such a long time. Ethel wrote and Mum answered, but it's not the same is it?

After two years Mum decided it was safe to have us home again. The lovely people who had taken care of us bought me the largest fire engine, turntable, lights and ladders. I carried that fire engine all the way from Colne to Bradford.

Mum just lived to see the end of the war. What a decision for any parent to have to make – to send the children away.

Peter Ridsdale. Inkersall

Billeting the boys

At the end of 1940 mass evacuation was ordered from London and the big cities. My Father's school landed up in Tredegar. Dad had to find accommodation for his party. Kindly ladies surveyed the children and seized on the little girls who hopefully would be no trouble. No one seemed to be interested in the older boys who might be a problem. Dad had difficulty trying to find accommodation for two boys who had nits. The local preacher pleaded "Give them to me, boyo, I'll pray over them!" "Pray over them," said Dad. "What they need is a good dose of Lysol!"

Enid Edwards. Chesterfield

Several evacuations

I was evacuated from London with the County High School for Girls, Ilford on 1 September 1939. We were taken by train to Ipswich and shared the Northgate Grammar School building. By May 1940 that area was presumably thought too dangerous, although I don't remember air raids, and we were re-evacuated to south Wales. This was again by train and unlike our arrival in Ipswich this time we were greeted by a cheering crowd. I remember visiting a farm where I saw a fox, nursed a lamb, had a ride on a carthorse and milked a cow. I had some of the warm milk straight from the milking.

The first week I stayed at a small pit village, Blaengaru, at the head of a valley. It hadn't a school big enough so we were moved to Aberdare. In the meantime my Father had been evacuated with the Civil Service to Harrogate where I joined him in December 1940 and attended a co-educational grammar school.

I have since read so many sad tales of children being traumatised by their evacuation experiences. I can only presume that they were the very young ones who didn't understand what was happening to them and needed to wear luggage labels. I'm fairly certain that my classmates and I didn't have them, perhaps because we were from a secondary school and therefore older.

I don't remember being unhappy even in the worst of my seven billets and I have good memories of two in particular. The last one in Ipswich introduced me to coffee, which I have loved ever since. The last one in Aberdare gave me a taste for bilberry tart and cream that I had never had before. We were able to pick the bilberries on the local mountainside. I was delighted to find when I came to Chesterfield that I could again pick them locally and even buy them in the shops in season.

Joyce Smith. Wingerworth

Evacuees on the march

The Evacuee Window, Sudbury

The window at All Saints' Parish Church, Sudbury, Derbyshire (shown in the coloured pictures) was designed and handmade by Michael Stokes. It was commissioned by a small group of evacuees from Manchester, and presented to the community during the first year of this Millennium, as an expression of their thanks and gratitude for the protection and affection they received during the war years. The inscription reads: "I was a stranger and you took me in".

Helen Nightingale. Holymoorside

Air raid shelters and wardens

Steel-built Anderson shelters were constructed in back gardens all over the country, some situated underground, others well sand-bagged. Morrison shelters were designed for erection indoors. Anderson shelters dating from the war still survive as garden sheds. Some families decided on places in the house where they would shelter – under the stairs, in the cellar or in the pantry, rather than dash for the cold, damp shelter. There were communal shelters in cities. London underground stations were used as shelters during the blitz and it became a nightly ritual to take blankets, sleeping bags and pillows, food and drink and, of course, your gas mask, to sleep in the shelter. Men and women came home from their jobs prepared to spend the night as wardens patrolling the streets, supervising air raid procedures, checking that no lights were showing, keeping order and taking whatever action was necessary to fight fires or give assistance.

Air raid wardens

Air raid wardens were on standby for any incident and to check for any chinks of light. Schools and offices had to have fire watchers (members of staff) on duty every night, prepared to put out fires started by incendiary bombs with buckets of water and stirrup pumps. Our elder brother was fire watching, at the office in Hull where he worked, on his eighteenth birthday, when one of the fiercest raids on the city took place.

Dinah Evans. Scarborough

A 'cuppa'

We were warned of air raids by a siren sited in the middle of the Crescent. The ARP wardens visited – I suspect for the usual 'cuppa' after they had been 'playing trains', that is, blowing whistles around the area. That was my Mother's theory anyway.

Frances Showell. Holymoorside

A potential target

My family lived on King Street, off Derby Road, the main route from Derby to Sheffield and the industrial North. Chesterfield Tube Works and Brian Donkin's, both important manufacturers of munitions, were only half a mile from our house. Horn's Bridge, a main intersection of road and rail routes north/south and east/west was a little further along Derby Road with Markham's works close by. All were targets for bombing raids.

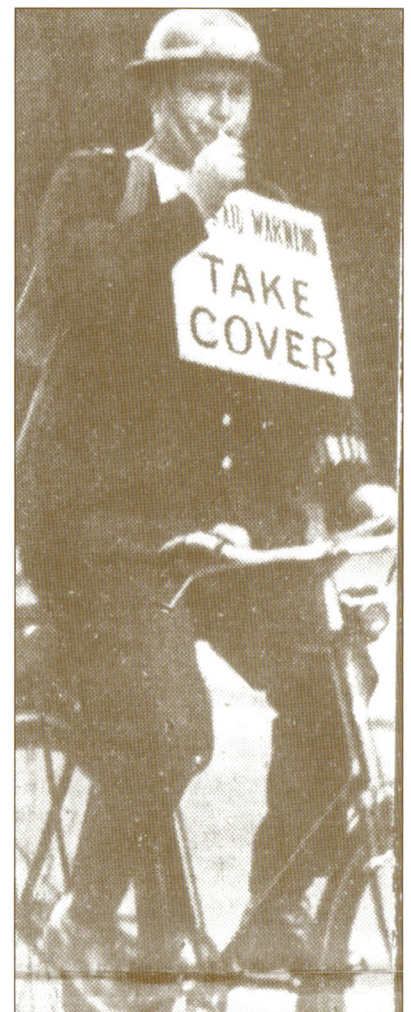

Air raid warden

Our Anderson shelter was barely 10 feet away from the back door and always seemed to be ankle-deep in water. I was born as war broke out so my memories are minimal. I don't think we ever went into our shelter though I remember playing in front of it. Perhaps Mum preferred the communal one on the local school field. I do remember the joy when it was demolished and the area became a garden again.

Helen Nightingale. Holymoorside

Making the shelter

My Dad started digging a big hole in the back yard. He said it was for the air raid shelter. The hole got deeper until I couldn't see over the edge if I stood in it. As it got deeper we found all kinds of interesting things in the ground, including old coins. Then some sheets of metal were fitted into the hole and fastened together so that it was like a little house below ground with just the curved roof sticking above the plants in the garden. It would be a safe place for us to sleep if the bombs came, my Dad said.

Peter Nightingale. Toronto

Playing in front of the shelter

Draining the shelter

My Grandfather dug a site for a shelter in the lawn in the back garden that promptly filled with water. Mr Proctor next door, who kept free-range poultry, suggested that together they should tunnel into the bank side, under one of his feed sheds, to drain the water. It was a very cosy shelter with old piano sconces to hold candles on the wooden uprights. The cats, kept to keep the mice down in the feed store, joined us. They purred so loudly we couldn't hear the planes overhead.

Frances Showell. Holymoorside

Volunteer wardens

Wardens were in charge of people in their designated area of the village. They asked us to inform them where we would take shelter during an air raid, so they would know where to start digging if a bomb hit our house and we were buried there. Mother thought the pantry under the stairs would be the safest place but I disagreed as the gas and electricity meters were there. It was, however, where we went when the air raid sirens wailed. Our neighbour's husband was a warden and he had to report for duty when the alarm sounded, so his wife joined us in the rather small pantry.

Joan Baltare (nee Nightingale). Vancouver

Air raid sirens

I was just falling off to sleep when the air raid siren went. The hooter from the factory round the corner sent up a long, loud wail, stayed poised on the top note for a second or two before descending to the bottom note and then up again. This miserable, mournful noise continued up and down for two minutes. We gathered once more in the dining room in our nightclothes with jumpers and cardigans on top. We sat in silence, each holding our little cardboard gas mask box on our knees. Some twenty minutes later the siren's wail rent the silence again. This time it stayed on the top note for a couple of minutes, before fading away. "That's the all-clear," said Dad, "we can all go back to bed again."

Sheila Lacey. Dronfield

Top to toe

The air raid shelter had a door at garden level and steps that went underground to a small room with a roof of 6 inch thick reinforced concrete and a man-hole cover as an escape hatch. It had two wide bunk beds. My brother and I slept top to toe in the upper berth, our parents in the lower. Grandpa, who lived with us, refused to leave his own bed. During the Sheffield blitz we heard many planes going over. You learnt to recognise the sound of the enemy planes by their engine note. Single planes going home and dropping their bombs indiscriminately were the most scary, the ground shaking as they exploded.

Jean Birkumshaw. Holymoorside

WHO'S THAT STRANGER, MOTHER DEAR?

LOOK, HE KNOWS US AIN'T HE QUEER?

DON'T BE FOOLISH, DON'T TALK WILD –

– THAT'S YOUR FATHER, DARLING CHILD!

THAT MY FATHER, NO SUCH THING!

FATHER DIED, YOU KNOW, LAST SPRING.

NO, FATE WAS NOT QUITE SO HARD –

– FATHER JUST JOINED THE HOME GUARD

SO NOW NO LONGER NEED WE GRIEVE,

FATHER'S GOT A FORTNIGHTS LEAVE!

Homework in the shelter

Air raid shelters were provided at school and at home. We had a concrete Anderson shelter in the garden. It was about six feet square and six of us slept there in two bunk beds, an easy chair and a pram. There was a period when there were air raid warnings every night, from early evening until early morning (because we were on the flight path to inland cities) and we took to doing our homework in the shelter and going to bed there as a matter of course. With no streetlights we would see wonderful starry skies at night, and glorious sunrises when we went back into the house in the morning. There was an anti-aircraft gun emplacement at the end of our street and the noise from that was much louder than that from any bomb near us. My sister and I were more bothered by the spiders and the drips from condensation on the ceiling! But it was many years before the wail of an air raid siren ceased to give me butterflies in the stomach. The 'all-clear' was a much more reassuring sound.

Dinah Evans. Scarborough

Behind the sofa

The daytime was ok but when darkness fell, this was something different. Sirens wailed, the blackout, then aircraft overhead which were deafening. We just hoped they were ours. We had no air raid shelter so it was out of bed, downstairs, not forgetting the little square box, and settle behind the sofa where Ethel and I attempted a large jig-saw puzzle, 'Knights Castile Soap'. I will never forget it.

Peter Ridsdale. Inkersall

Our cellar

Our house had a cellar to which the air raid wardens had an entry. There they kept their dartboard and were there nearly every night. We cleared the shelves of what had been a bottle store to use the cellar as our shelter. Grandmother came to live with us. She was elderly and had to be helped down the stairs into the cellar to sleep on the shelves.

Running to the shelter

Peter Robson. Chesterfield

Air raid shelter
- now a garden shed

Humour

For some reason we didn't qualify for an Anderson shelter. It was probably a mixed blessing, as they got very damp. Instead we crouched under the stairs. This lasted about nine months but the lack of sleep was telling on all of us. We were then offered space in my school shelter where a least we could lie down on slatted seating. We got our humour where we could. A prankster left us a present, a sweet packet on the floor and as we bent to pick it up, it moved. John solved the mystery by bravely undoing the top and out popped a toad.

Enid Edwards. Walton

Ask for shelter

My brother and I used to walk to school and we had strict instructions that if there was an air raid warning we had to go to the nearest house, knock at the door and ask if we could come in.

Peter Robson. Chesterfield

Outside in the raid

During the bombing of Sheffield I went to the cinema in the village with a friend. During the film the sirens sounded the alert. As usual there was an announcement that a raid was expected and that there would be a five-minute break so that anybody that wanted could leave, and then the film would continue. We decided to stay. When we came out, the bombing of Sheffield was at its height. There were aircraft overhead and we could hear the explosions and see the flashes of light and the glow of fires. We ran home as fast as we could to be met by my brother-in-law wearing a steel helmet and carrying a bucket of sand to deal with incendiary bombs. He wasn't pleased to see us outside. He rushed us home and put us in the shelter. It was a small shelter and already quite crowded. It was so well built that it is still there, under the concrete at the edge of the garden.

A one-ton Herman bomb landed in the village but luckily did not explode. It wasn't unearthed until 1977. A friend heard a bomb coming down and jumped over a wall for shelter. It was another that didn't go off and as far as he knows it is still there.

Ruby Wilkinson. Beighton

17

Civil Defence

The phoney war lasted well into 1940 but the fall of France and the evacuation of British forces from Dunkirk prompted a real fear of invasion. The AFS (Auxiliary Fire Service), ARP (Air Raid Precautions) and the Messenger Service were set up for civil defence and in May 1940 the War Minister (Anthony Eden) called for a new defence force to be established. It was originally known as the LDV (Local Defence Volunteers). Recruits had to be between 17 and 65 years of age and 'capable of free movement'. The response was immense and the force was soon renamed the Home Guard.

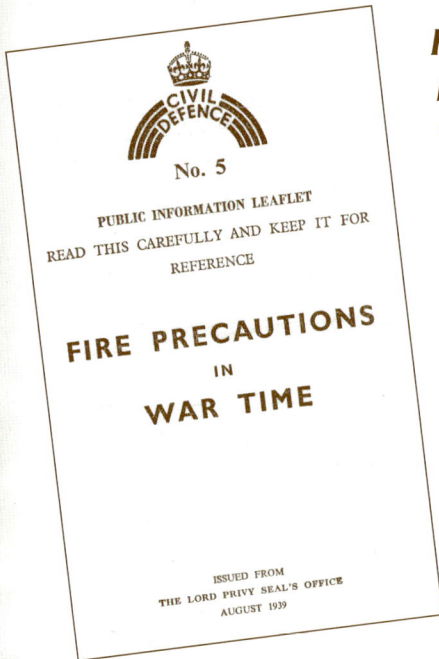

CIVIL DEFENCE

No. 5

PUBLIC INFORMATION LEAFLET

READ THIS CAREFULLY AND KEEP IT FOR REFERENCE

FIRE PRECAUTIONS
IN
WAR TIME

ISSUED FROM
THE LORD PRIVY SEAL'S OFFICE
AUGUST 1939

CD Leaflet No. 5

Fire precautions

It is probable that in an air attack an enemy would make use of bombs .... to destroy property and create panic. In Civil Defence everybody has a part to play.

Civil Defence Leaflet No 5

Invasion?

After Dunkirk the announcer on the wireless was reading the news. "Hitler's army is poised for the invasion of Britain". I wondered, if the Germans had spread so quickly through France, how long would it take to do the same to Britain? All able-bodied men at home had been asked to enrol as Local Defence Volunteers (soon called the Home Guard) to protect the streets and houses of their local community when the unthinkable happened. Not that it was unthinkable – everyone thought it would happen.

Sheila Lacey. Dronfield

Auxiliary Fire Service

My mates and I were on call as part time members of the Auxiliary Fire Service (AFS). One night we received an emergency call from Nottingham to report immediately with our four-man pump as cover because all other appliances had been sent to help with the Coventry blitz. We rang to say that for that night we only had three-man cover but that we would come straight away. We dashed out, hitched on the pump and climbed into the vehicle only to realise that there was no one in the driver's seat. Ted the driver was off. We had to call in to send another driver. This sort of thing used to happen frequently. We can laugh at it now but it didn't look too good at the time.

Another time we were called to Nottingham with our pump for an exercise. There were big

"I hope you don't mind him watching you. It's so difficult to get toys to amuse him nowadays."

auxiliary water tanks by the castle ready for air raids. These were fed by cast iron pipes laid in the gutter, leading from a pump by the river. This was started to top up the water tanks. However, there was no means of communication with the pump and the tanks started to overflow. There were few drains by the castle and water started to flow into houses. We were ordered to run our hoses into any drain we could find until a message could be got to the river. Real Dad's Army stuff.

Eric Dove. Chesterfield

The Messenger Service

I was a member of the Messenger Service, a small section of the Civil Defence, boys and girls who wanted to do their bit but had no idea how to do it. We learned bit by bit and, I like to think, improved on the way. Fortunately we were not called upon to do any daring deeds and had the general public known about our efforts, I doubt if it would have inspired confidence. There's not much you can do with a bicycle, note pad and pencil.

K. Crossland. Somersall

ARP Messenger

During the war I was a Chesterfield Grammar School boy and also an ARP Messenger, later a Civil Defence Messenger. Eventually at 16 I became a motorcycle messenger on BSA and Matchless machines working from E Sector that was mainly Brampton. The nearest ARP centre was at Loggins garage. ARP wardens were awarded badges for stirrup pump training, covering phosphorus bombs with sand, resuscitation and first aid.

Harry Husband. Walton

Incendiary bomb

An incendiary bomb dropped near the railway. We had an allotment nearby and my Mother was most indignant that her precious Brussels sprout plants were uprooted to beat out the fire. It didn't help that my Father was an ARP warden and probably one of the culprits.

Margaret Copley. Holymoorside

Joining up

Early in the war I reported for work at the Post Office headquarters to work as a teleprinter operator. This was the telegram centre of the city. Telegrams from all over the country came on long strips of paper through a hole at the side of the keyboard. These had to be cut and stuck onto the correct form, then put on a moving table ready for delivery. Telegraph boys would collect the sorted messages and deliver them by bicycle.

I worked for the Lord Mayor's 'Comforts Fund' sending parcels to any soldier from the county whose name had been sent in. All members of the forces from our area were allowed one parcel every six months. After a short time I knew the whereabouts of practically every Army and Air Force station in the country – classified information!

In 1943 I joined the ATS (Auxiliary Training Service) after a medical examination. I was issued with my pay book, identification papers and uniform. I was kitted out with two sets of everything, including nightwear, underclothes and even corsets. Regulations on appearance were strict. Skirts had to be one inch below the knee, no higher, no lower. Hair must not touch the collar, shoes had to shine and jackets buttoned and always worn except in hot weather, when permission may be given not to wear them. In that case shirtsleeves had to be rolled up, but rolled inwards rather than outward.

Sheila Lacey. Dronfield

Memories of Calow Home Guard

Arthur Lowe as
Captain Mainwaring

A civilian army was needed and the LDV (Local Defence Volunteers) was formed in May 1940 (or, as some wit named them, the Look, Duck and Vanish brigade!) In July 1940, the name was changed to the Home Guard and Calow's own Dad's Army was formed. There was no shortage of volunteers and the Calow platoon had some forty members. In charge, and responsible for the organisation, was Father Handford, Vicar of St Peter's, their own Captain Mainwaring (remember the TV series Dad's Army?) A tallish man, he was unlike the latter in build.

Volunteers came from all walks of life, miners, farm workers, clerks, those too young and those too old to join the armed forces. Many of the older men, including the Vicar and my Father, Percy Vardy, had already seen service in WWI, some had seen trench warfare and the younger members were often senior Scouts.

To begin with, they had no uniforms and no weapons; later they were issued with khaki armbands bearing the initials LDV. Then, they had denim battle dress and an issue of six rifles used by Canadian troops in WWI. Later still, they had proper khaki battle dress complete with greatcoats, boots, ankle protectors, steel helmets, rifles and bayonets. The Vicararge was the arsenal and the Vicar was apparently delighted when they received a machine gun!

These men had full-time jobs and often little sleep; they trained in their own time and prepared to defend their country. The elderly and retired sacrificed what should have been their peaceful years to do the same. In addition, each member had to do one night's guard duty each week from 10 p.m. to 6 a.m. for which they received the princely sum of one shilling and six pence. The guard hut was on a hill in one of Mr Thompson's fields; a path led down across the field to Lodge Farm and down the drive to the main road where, opposite, stood the White Hart.

Calow School was the place where they assembled once a week (Monday evening if I remember correctly). Here in the school yard they marched and drilled and in the classrooms had lectures. Rifle practice took place behind the vicarage and at Hardwick Hall, where they also had bayonet practice and the throwing of hand grenades. Here, they went on assault courses, which some of the older men found gruelling. Occasionally, there would be a mock battle; once, the Home Guard launched an attack on Staveley Works, which was defended by regular soldiers. The Home Guard was wiped out!

Many amusing stories were told, such as the time they were on manoeuvres and some of the men were concealed in the ditches on either side of Church Lane. In those days, the left hand side of the road facing the church, from Blacksmith's Lane to the few houses at the top, were all Proctor's rose gardens and on the right, there were fields belonging to Mr Butler, a farmer. Apparently, one or two housewives saw the men and took them cups of tea, which they accepted. Captain Handford was furious and said they had ruined the exercise, the enemy now knew their exact wherabouts!

Personal memories include my Mother stitching stripes on Dad's uniform – he had two. There were entertaining evenings, when the table would be moved back, the rug rolled up and Dad would practice his crawls. The one I remember is the tiger crawl. My Mother would be laughing and ask him to repeat the performance, to which he would say "This isn't a game you know, there is a war on". He would tell me to use the blunt end of a pencil and with a list of dots and dashes, I would tap out the Morse code for him to decipher.

One morning, on getting up for school, my Mother told me to take him a mug of tea as he was on guard. I protested, saying by the time I had reached the guard hut at the top of Thompson's fields, what little tea that would be left in the mug would be cold. She said, "He isn't at the guard hut, he is over the wall in the corner." (It is now The White Hart car park but at the time it was rough land belonging to the three White Hart cottages.) I went out and Dad's head appeared, twigs and leaves in the netting of his steel helmet and dirt on his face. It didn't appear strange at the time but I don't know to this day what he was doing there – maybe guarding the White Hart?

Patricia Mary Cooper (nee Vardy). Calow

'Per ardua ad astra'

My brother, who lived in Brampton, joined the Home Guard in 1942 when he was sixteen. There were men from all around the Chesterfield district. They had to go on assault courses just like those in the army. They had a firing range with fixed targets for anti-tank weapons, one called the 'block buster'. One of the jobs they had to do was to dig trenches at major road junctions on the outskirts of Chesterfield.

He received his calling-up papers for either Bomber Crew, Submarines or Navy. He chose aircrew. After the war he stayed on in the RAF becoming Air Vice Marshall and was awarded the Order of the Bath.

A. M. Randall. Somersall

Towards the end

The ack-ack gun in the vicinity of Ford Valley, south of Sheffield, was now silent. The quarter inch canopy over my bed had been removed. Mother had said that it was there to protect me should a bomb fall on the house. The Fire Watchers' armbands had been removed and the blue, steel helmets handed in. They ceased to congregate in our kitchen and the cribbage board had been put away. The Home Guard had abandoned operations in our street with their bren-guns at the ready. We used to fire at them with our homemade wooden pistols and the Sergeant would chase us, calling out, "Now bugger off".

Barry Woodcock. Chesterfield

Home Guard unit

Air raids

Between the summer of 1940, when the Battle of Britain began, and the spring of 1941, Britain was subjected to the blitz, a sustained assault of bombing. Large cities were among the principal targets. Raids were made on the same areas for several nights running to destroy industry and docks and to weaken the resolve of the people. Nearly 2000 people were killed in the first night of the blitz on London on Saturday, 7 September 1940. Even country districts suffered if they were near to an industrial or military centre or on the flight path of enemy aircraft. Many bombs were dropped indiscriminately. The county of Kent became known as 'bomb alley' as it lay on the flight path to London. The attacks became a part of everyday life and each day people emerged from the shelters to continue their lives and jobs.

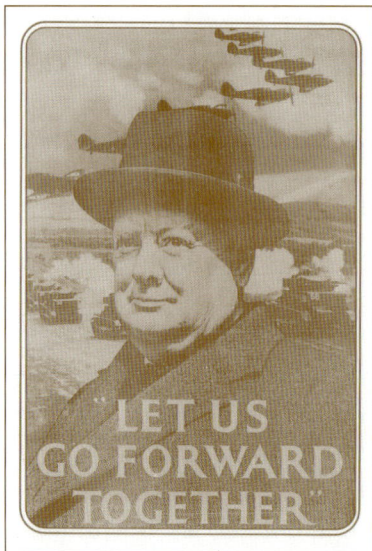

Wartime poster

Mr Winston Churchill

Churchill spoke directly to the people. In September 1940 he witnessed the destruction in the East End of London when 300 people were killed and over 1300 injured. People sitting around their bakelite wireless sets heard these characteristically challenging words:

"These cruel, wanton, indiscriminate bombings of London are, of course, a part of Hitler's invasion plans. He hopes, by killing large numbers of civilians, women and children, that he will terrorise and cow the people of this mighty, imperial city."

Anon

The first bombing of Sheffield

It was a dark night when Sheffield was bombed for the first time. There was a terrific explosion and the sky was ablaze from the fires. My uncle had built a bomb shelter in his garden close by, just a hole in the ground covered with corrugated iron and earth. We all dashed to it, finishing up in about a foot of water, my uncle's comment being "Bugger this, we may as well die from the bombs as die from pneumonia."

Graham Anthony. Chesterfield

"Ooh"

The Battle of Britain

We lived in Rainham, south east Essex just outside the greater London area and three miles from the perimeter of RAF Hornchurch Fighter Station. The attack by the German air force began with attempts to wipe out RAF fighters on their airfields. It started for us when the sirens went and within minutes Hornchurch was under attack. We were in the shelter very quickly and only heard loud bangs and the earth shook (even today the sound of air raid sirens in war films brings back that tummy-turning feeling). We came up from the shelter after the attack and smoke was coming from various parts of the airfield. Hornchurch was damaged but not completely out of action. Soon Spitfires and Hurricanes began to return from the air fights, some obviously damaged, some with spluttering engines. We could never tell what our losses were. If you counted them out when they flew over our bungalow, they came back a different way.

The attacks became part of everyday life. We even stood outside our shelter and cheered when an enemy aeroplane went into a dive with smoke pouring from the engine, sometimes turning into a groan when it was recognised as one of ours. We could clearly see the silver shapes of planes in the sky with condensation trails streaming behind them. We would watch until shrapnel or debris began to ping off the rooftops, then it was time to shelter.

Peter Rothwell. Walton

The bombing of Coventry

For me the war started in the autumn of 1940 with the bombing of Coventry. After months of intermittent bombing we had been forced to move to the comparative safety of Kenilworth six miles from the city centre. The schools had been closed, there was an increasing number of empty desks, sweets were rationed, buses didn't run, we were constantly woken at night and there was no playing in the park which was full of barrage balloons like large elephants. From Kenilworth we could see the night-time bombing of Coventry and hear the distant crump of exploding bombs as we dashed to the air raid shelter, with our bundles of bedding, thermos, sandwiches and board games, all tangled with the string of the gas mask box, while making way for fire engines and ambulances on their way to Coventry. We spent whole nights in the cold and smelly brick shelter, hearing the noise and feeling the vibration of the exploding bombs.

When we emerged from the shelter we were confronted by a steady stream of families leaving the city in cars or on foot, wearily carrying hastily gathered bundles of belongings or pushing prams with strangely quiet children holding their parents' hands.

Adrian Marsden-Jones. Holymoorside

The bombing of Holymoorside

I remember practising diving under the kitchen table in case a bomb was dropped. When the bombs were dropped at Bage Hill – I was promptly sick. The blast was felt at home, in the Crescent, and the roof was showered in what sounded like a load of cinders being emptied on it. In that incident a cow was killed and the stick of five bombs down 'Little Blackpool' also killed a cow. These, I believe, were the only casualties in the village. The moors were on fire and burned for months. We understood that they were left to burn to distract bombers from the industry in Chesterfield and Sheffield.

Frances Showell,. Holymoorside

Bombs in Holymoorside

There was some bombing. The first bomb was a high explosive that fell across the valley. It shook our house the way you would shake out a sack. Before that I had thought it was a safe refuge. The most frightening was the string of screaming bombs that landed about fifty metres from our house. I heard them start to scream far away then get louder and closer. Finally they were so loud that I was sure they were coming directly at me. I was as good as dead I thought, having heard the previous explosion. It was a relief to hear them explode and know that 'my number wasn't on that one', as my Mother had taught us to say. Then there were time bombs. They had fallen we knew, but where exactly we didn't know - for a while.

Peter Nightingale. Toronto

Misleading the enemy

During the bombing, bins full of oily rags were lit all along Derby Road, creating clouds of oily black smoke over the town. You had to crouch low to find fresh air. Bonfires were also lit on the racecourse to mislead the bombers.

Eric Dove. Ashgate

Crater

I grew up in Sussex in a village called Keymer under the Downs. We could hear the sirens warning of approaching enemy aircraft but only once were we troubled by enemy action. One night an explosion rattled our windows and the next day the whole village gathered to marvel at a crater in the middle of a local farmer's field. The cows were interested too.

Daphne Isherwood. Tibshelf

'Observer Corps'

As a youngster during the war, I lived near the Thames estuary. The German bombers used the river as a flight path to London and the docks. There were fighter stations, such as Hornchurch, on the Essex coast and many bombers turned back and jettisoned their bombs indiscriminately in their haste to get home safely.

Our dog, frightened by the deafening explosions, became familiar with the distinctive drone of the German bombers and would hide under the settee. We therefore had advance warning of a raid long before the sirens sounded. He could clearly distinguish between our fighters and the enemy bombers.

We were fortunate to have a Morrison shelter inside that was dry enough to store food and bedding. The Anderson shelters, dug into the ground, were dreadfully damp, so that clothes, food and bedding had to be carried in and out. No time to make a drink or go back for anything.

David King. Renishaw

Crashed plane on Pocknedge Lane

A light aircraft crashed near Farmer White's on Pocknedge Lane. Luckily the airmen could crawl out of it but had to face Mr White with his shotgun. They were able to convince him they were on his side and were picked up. The wreckage was loaded on a flatbed and pulled down the lane to be parked outside our house. Soldiers were brought in to guard it. My aunt and uncle were staying with us as the bombing around their home in London was very heavy. Uncle, a WWI veteran, persuaded the soldiers to come into the house from the cold and have a cup of hot tea. Unfortunately, their sergeant arrived while they were inside and he wasn't very happy. The plane was moved the next day.

Joan Baltare (nee Nightingale). Vancouver

Public air raid shelter sign

The blitz

The London blitz, the nightly air raids on the City, started around the middle of September 1940 and continued until May 1941 when Hitler withdrew his squadrons of bombers to attack Russia. People no longer waited for the sirens but went straight to the shelter as soon as darkness fell. The three of us collected food for the night and made sure we had the Monopoly board, draughts, candles, and gas masks. We had installed electricity but if the power supply failed there was no light or radio. We stayed there until daylight but if there were any explosions that sounded close we would pop out during a quiet spell to see if the bungalow was still standing and that there was no burning incendiary device. If you heard the scream of a falling bomb but no explosion, you were then concerned about unexploded bombs.

One night a raid started in the evening when I was on my way home. The street was full of puddles reflecting the flashes of bombs and gunfire. It must have been like that at the Somme. I can't remember what the Olympic record was for the 100 yards but I beat it easily when I panicked and ran for home and shelter.

The Jerries dropped sea mines aimed at the river but if they fell on land they caused an enormous amount of damage. On one occasion I went on my bike to collect the evening papers for my paper round and all my usual roads were closed with UXB (unexploded bomb) notices. There was suddenly an almighty bang and glass, tiles, bricks and other debris began to fall. I got off the bike and down behind the fence as quickly as I could. A mine had been hanging by its parachute from the corner of a roof and as the bomb disposal officers had gone to diffuse it, it had exploded killing them both.

Peter Rothwell. Chesterfield

In the blackout

One night I was walking home in the blackout and bumped into an old man. "Sorry, sorry," I said. "Where are you going?" he asked.

"Canning Circus."

"Well so am I," he replied. "Just keep hold of my arm, I can get there faster than you, I'm used to it and these conditions suit me."

"What do you mean?"

"Well there aren't many people about – they don't go out if they don't have to. The roads are clear and I'm blind, so it's always dark to me!"

Eric Dove. Ashgate

Crepe-soled shoes

When the spongy crepe-soled shoes were first introduced, my Mother and I were walking home in the blackout. We heard someone approaching with heavy footsteps and knew they could neither hear nor see us. Quickly Mother said "Pip-pip" to save us being crashed into. I don't remember the reaction – I just hope he didn't have a heart attack!

Frances Showell. Holymoorside

Helping the bus driver

Coming out of work in the winter darkness and the blackout there was always a rush for the buses – no queues just a crush with each person trying to get on their own bus. One night we had a driver who didn't know the route. It was very difficult for him with no streetlights, no cat's eyes in those days and only tiny lights on his bus to drive by. We managed by each person as they came near to their stop getting up to guide the driver. It must have been a nightmare for the driver but he got us home.

Ruby Wilkinson. Beighton

A memory of the blitz in London.

At the back of our row of terraced houses was a garment factory. The access drive of the factory was easy to get to through our back garden. Attached to the factory was a surface shelter that was built for the workers. At night it was available for local residents.

At the height of the blitz we used this shelter, along with other residents. Shelters were not the most comfortable places. Ventilation was limited and they always felt damp, and if a lot of people were in there, they smelt of sweat, socks and other things. They were not silent places either - crying, adults as well as children, snoring, conversation and sometimes arguments.

On this particular night, the raid seemed very heavy, the sound of aircraft engines was endless. The noise from anti - aircraft guns was sometimes deafening and the bombs, when they dropped, could be felt through the ground as much as heard.

The first memorable bomb that night was a screamer. It seemed that on some bombs, a siren was fitted so that as it descended it screamed. It was very frightening, which I suppose was the intention. As the scream of the bomb became louder and louder all conversation stopped, then the screaming stopped, the ground shook, there was an enormous bang, and we knew that we were safe. Next day we learnt that this particular bomb had hit a block of flats in Stoke Newington High Street called Coronation Buildings, less than a quarter of a mile away. It had gone through four floors, through the basement, where hundreds of people were sheltering, and had blown up underneath in the gas and water main. Many were dead, the high street was closed for two days as the Pioneer Corps cleared up the mess.

Later, close outside, there was a sound like a train, a series of bangs as if a train were going over points, then silence. George, an old man, the Warden of the shelter, went outside to see what had happened, but in the dark he could see nothing. In the morning we left the shelter and saw in a large tree, some fifty yards away, a cylinder hanging on a lot of strings. The cylinder seemed very large and it was a little while before people worked out what it was. It was a land mine, meant to come down slowly on a parachute and explode either on impact or at some level above the ground.

If it had exploded, we would have been dead. But it didn't, so I am here to write about it. Someone did lose their life in trying to defuse it, a naval bomb disposal officer. It exploded while he was working on it. In the meantime we, and many others in the area, had been evacuated to a church hall and to communal living, which I hated. The damage caused was extensive, half the street was blown away. The roof of our house was gone and all the windows blown in. Our dog had vanished, we were forbidden to take him to the church hall and in the time available to us we had no time to do anything with him but leave him in the house.

About a week later we were back in our house with tarpaulin on the roof and most of the windows repaired. The dog was gone and we never saw it again.

After cleaning up the glass, it was almost normal. Except the bombing did not stop. We were lucky; many were not.

Alex Simpson. Holymoorside

Attack on London Docks

On my sister's birthday a devastating attack took place on the London Docks. The docks were ablaze from end to end – warehouses, houses, sugar, wood, food, spices – everything was on fire and huge palls of smoke billowed from the West Ham, Canning Town and Poplar areas. The fire went on for days. I can remember cycling along New Road, Dagenham where exhausted AFS fire crews from all parts of the country were sleeping on their trailers, or on the pavement, with blackened faces, too tired to clean up before going back to the fires. One morning on my paper round a policeman stepped out from behind a telephone kiosk and stopped me. I thought I was going to get ticked off for being out before the all clear sounded. Not a bit of it, he wanted to know if I had a permit from school to do a paper round.

Peter Rothwell. Walton

The three-day fire

I lived in Edgeware, north west of London. During raids I can remember trailing down the garden clutching garments for warmth, also drinks and my gas mask. I still hate the sound of sirens. I had to go to hospital, raids or no raids, as I suffered from rickets. My Father was an air raid warden at night. I can still see in my mind's eye the city burning all night in the three-day fire that my Father worked on for two days and, when he came home, I can still remember him, a very shaken man, weeping at the sight of exhausted firemen asleep in the gutter, because they were at the end of their conscious effort.

Ruth Robson. Chesterfield

Don't worry Granny

Air raids for a tiny child were experiences of fun rather than fear and I used to say "Don't worry, Granny, it's only the bombs" which in retrospect shows how little did I understand. During the daytime bombing, we were placed under the grand piano with the settee rolled in front of it. Mother would play music and sing to us under the piano. My Grandmother's sister lived 40 years after the war with shrapnel in her.

Ruth Robson. Chesterfield

V-1s

V-1 was the real name but everyone called them buzz bombs, because they made a buzzing sound different from that of an aeroplane. It was like an unmanned aeroplane packed with explosive and with a rocket instead of a tail plane. They were directed at London and when the rocket cut out they just dived on to the city making an explosion sufficient to destroy several houses or a whole factory. Many fell short and landed in Sussex. We used to go outside and watch them. If they kept going until they were overhead then they wouldn't land on you, but would fall a few miles further on. If the engine stopped when the buzz bomb was out to sea, then we ran for it! The air defences would go flat out to bring them down before they reached the coast. I saw one direct hit. It was high up over the sea coming towards us. It exploded into a gigantic ball of flame. We ran into the house and for a few seconds nothing happened, then there was a thundering roar, as it took time for the sound to reach us.

John Pratt. Holymoorside

Doodlebugs

V-1s were pilotless weapons consisting of an engine, a wing and an explosive. The Germans called them Victory Weapon 1, a weapon to terrorise the civilian population, but Londoners nicknamed them Doodlebugs. They were launched from inclined ramps in Northern France and the Lowlands. Once in the air they were difficult to stop. The ack-ack guns were moved from the outskirts of London to the coast to intercept them. They were always going to explode whether brought down by fighters, which could barely catch up with them, or when winged by gunfire. It was a weapon you could hear coming from a long way off. When the engine ran out of fuel you held your breath and took cover. The bomb might glide on for miles or fall straight to earth with an almighty bang. For many, this was too much and it took its toll on the nervous system. The area from the coast to London became known as bomb alley. This phase of the war took some adjusting to. But people did adjust and life continued once you learned what to do when the engine cut out.

Peter Rothwell. Chesterfield

Get up call

It was early on a sunny, Sunday morning. My brother and I were still in bed, when the shadow of a V-1 passed across the window. You could recognise it by the sound. At the same instant the engine noise stopped. My brother and I were down the stairs faster than we had ever been before. We heard the explosion a moment later, a few streets away.

Alex Simpson. Holymoorside

Shooting down Doodlebugs

My memories of war – blackout, the Council coming down the road sawing off railings, the pig bins, scrap metal, air raid shelters, going to the panto in Sheffield after the blitz, brown gum paper on the classroom windows. A vivid memory is of my Father who was called up in his late thirties and served in the Royal Artillery, shooting down Doodlebugs. When he came home on leave, he used to sit me on his knee and draw them, with the guns used to shoot them down.

Dad struck up a friendship with a gamekeeper from Norfolk. He was stationed in Chesterfield with a searchlight battalion billeted at Old Whittington. Uncle Ted, as we called him, used to take us down to the Nissen huts where they had silhouettes of aeroplanes on the ceiling so that they could recognise them in the searchlights. We stayed in Norfolk in a remote cottage about 2 miles from R.A.F. Swannington. There was no electricity, candles to bed, no running water, a pump was the only supply. We used to sit up in the bedroom watching the Mosquito aircraft taking off on night raids and at the same time watching barn owls raiding the nightlife. One day a Mosquito, returning from a mission, crashed in a cornfield and caught fire. We all rushed across the field as the fire tenders were coming from the camp. Sadly the aircrew perished. We found a forage cap and kept it as a souvenir, although I believe it could have belonged to the fire crew.

John Cuttriss. Newbold

V-2 rockets

When the Germans started firing V-2 rockets there was no warning. If you heard the bang you had survived, provided the debris or shrapnel didn't get you. It was from a V-2 that I had my closest escape. I was on my way to night school and had just passed a pub and a row of cottages when I heard the explosion. I took shelter behind a low garden wall until the debris stopped falling and everything settled down. Then I went back a hundred yards or so. The pub was a heap of rubble and many of the houses had gone. There was an awful smell of dust and smoke. Bodies lay around and people were coming out of the nearby houses, crying and shocked. I thought afterwards that the margin between life and death was a couple of minutes.

Rocket and flying bomb attacks continued right up until the Allied Forces invaded France and advanced into the Low Countries.

Peter Rothwell. Chesterfield

A close one

I remember getting up one morning to go to school. As I went downstairs I heard an aeroplane coming in very low, a clattering on the roof, and my Father shouting urgently "Get down, lie down" which I did. It was all over in a flash and we heard later that it was a German fighter returning to its base after escorting a bombing raid. It had dived to machine-gun the soldiers marching to Ashgate Drill Hall. Later, Dad found machine gun bullets in the roof guttering.

Jean Birkumshaw. Holymoorside

Wheeling out a V-1

Propaganda

The sirens went at 12.30 and the all clear at 2.30. At about 1.00 there was a lot of gunfire, then about twelve high explosive bombs fell. Damage to property was very considerable. When the BBC tells you 'little material damage has been done in the raid' it's just British propaganda. This time quite a lot was done.

Peter Robson. Chesterfield

A lucky escape

My Aunty Polly and Uncle Jack lived in Swansea, in a terrace of houses in Sketty over looking the bay. They had been subjected to continuous nights of bombing, the enemy aiming for the docks and oil refineries.

They had lost so many nights of sleep in the shelters through air raid warnings, many of them false alarms, that they decided one night they had had enough. Packing a thermos and sandwiches they set off for a walk along the beach. Clinging together for comfort they witnessed an astounding display of searchlights criss-crossing the night sky and bright flashes of ack-ack fire. The town was lit up by the glow of exploding bombs and burning buildings. They took shelter in a beach hut until the raid was over and then made their way home to the sound of fire engines and ambulances. They climbed the hill near home until stopped from going any further by air raid wardens and police because of burning buildings. They spent the rest of the night in the local school with frightened families and endless cups of tea. In the morning they were allowed home but all Aunty Polly and Uncle Jack could find was a pile of smouldering rubble. Their house and several neighbours' houses had received a direct hit by a land mine and no one else had survived.

There was a great feeling of relief that they had been spared but my Aunty and Uncle were so devastated by the experience and the loss of all their belongings, that they moved out into the country until after the war.

Adrian Marsden-Jones. Holymoorside

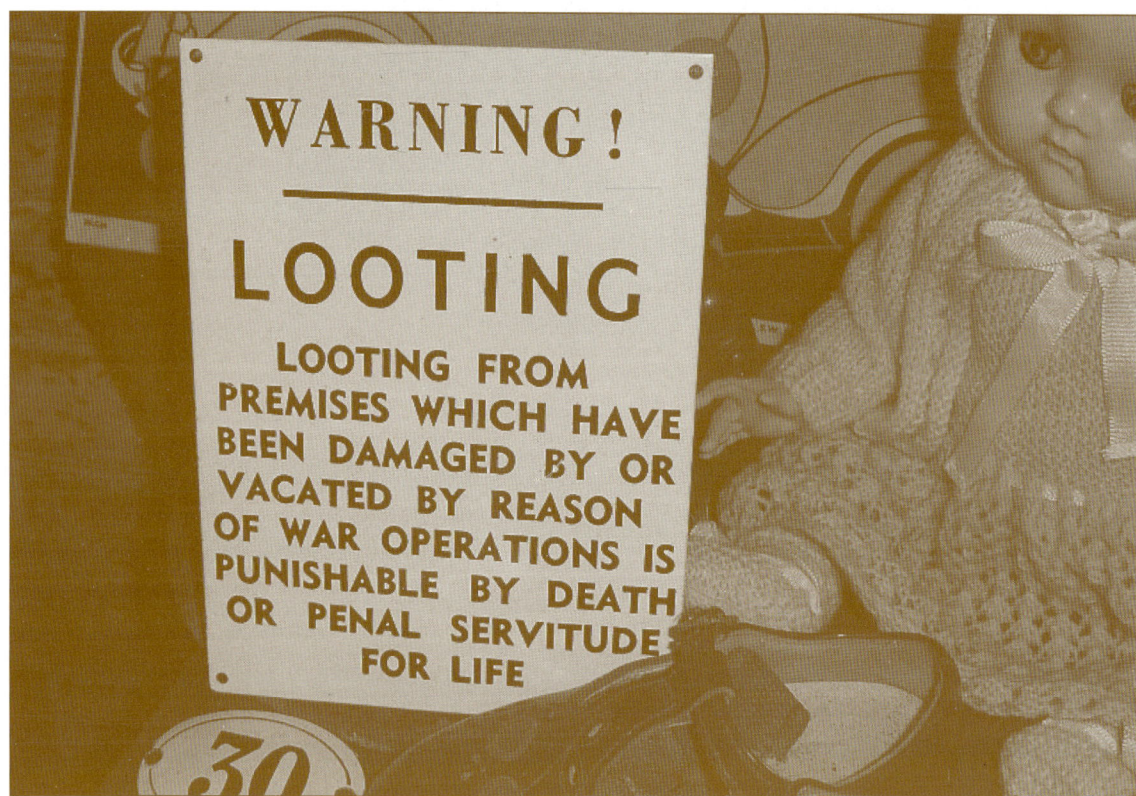

A stark warning

Shopping – food and rationing

Overseas imports were drastically cut in order to save currency reserves. Germany did its best to starve Britain into submission throughout the war. U-boats were sinking half a million tons of shipping every month at the height of the Battle of the Atlantic. Food rationing was introduced in stages and it was the law that householders must register with their local shops. Rationing was accepted, as most people agreed that it was fair and affected rich and poor alike. Nevertheless, queuing for food and making a little go a long way became a part of life. To boost vitamins in the diet, the Ministry of Health made daily milk, cod liver oil and orange juice available to all children. Householders dug up lawns and flowerbeds to grow vegetables in the Dig for Victory Campaign, and even berries were collected from the hedgerows to supplement vitamins.

Your food in wartime

Certain foods will be brought under a rationing scheme in the first instance applied to five foodstuffs – butcher's meat, bacon and ham, sugar, butter and margarine, and cooking fats.

Civil Defence Leaflet No 4

Drastic cuts in imports

Bacon, ham, butter and sugar were rationed in January 1940, followed by cooking fats, meat, tea, cheese, jam, eggs and sweets. The ration was supplemented with an allocation of points. Everyone received coupons worth 16 points per month that could be used for biscuits, cereal, tinned fish or fruit. Tinned salmon was rated as 16 points in December 1941, then 32 points in March 1942. Occasionally there was a little extra cheese or sausage that had to be queued for. People filled up with potatoes and vegetables.

CD Leaflet No. 4

Parks and gardens of stately homes were ploughed up to grow vegetables, especially potatoes, and cereals. Everybody with a garden was urged to grow vegetables and fruit. By 1943 there were nearly 1.5 million allotments being cultivated.

Recipes for potato dishes were given on the wireless. Potato cakes were made using mashed potato, a very little grated cheese, chopped onion and herbs. They were fried with a smear of national lard or sometimes we had beef dripping. Lord Woolton, the Minister of Food, gave his name to a pie. It consisted of potatoes, carrots, turnips and parsnips in an oatmeal stock, with a pastry crust and served with gravy.

For sweetening cakes and puddings, saccharine was dissolved in a drop of water and a little sugar was added. Camden tablets were used for preserving when bottling blackcurrants, damsons and plums. We never bottled rhubarb or raspberries. The Ministry of Food tried to cheer us up by announcing that raw carrot could be used to sweeten steamed puddings and cakes.

The meat ration was often poor quality. I remember Granny made a tasty hash of corned beef chopped up with carrots, potatoes, onions and herbs. SPAM (Supply Pressed American Meat) was a successful import. It looked and tasted like fresh meat.

Fish was never rationed but was in short supply, as the fishing grounds were infested with German submarines. Whale meat was served in schools and children had to get used to

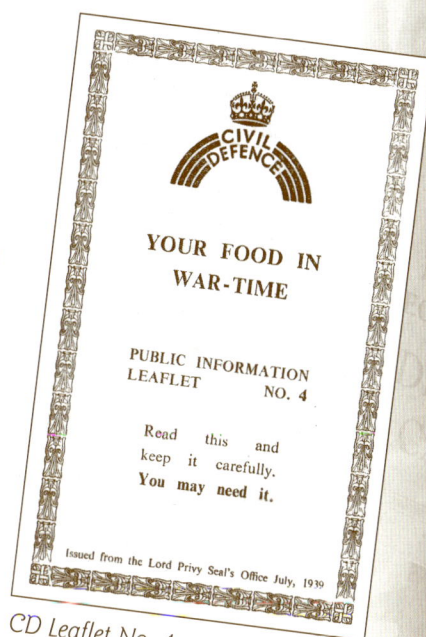

the fishy taste of whale meat Shepherd's pie. The nation never accepted whale meat.

We had eggs because Granny kept hens. They were fed on a special hen meal (for which coupons were required) mixed with a little water. The hens were free to roam and to eat grubs and grit. There was an Egg Marketing Board and eggs were collected weekly.

The Radio Doctor spoke every week telling us how to keep healthy. All young children were given cod liver oil, concentrated orange juice and National Dried Milk. Shopping and thinking up meals for families must have been a nightmare for women.

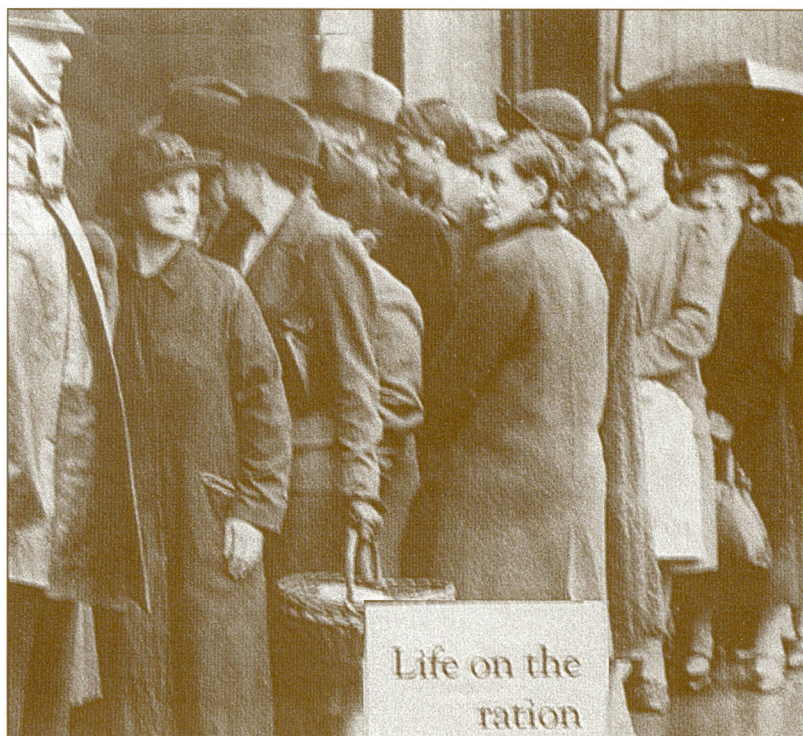

Housewives queue for food

E. Mary Wardale. Holymoorside

The Radio Doctor Says:

'If I were allowed to say only three things on the Kitchen Front, I should say eat some raw green vegetables every day, I should praise milk and more milk and I should preach the virtues of the food which contains so much nutriment—cheese.'

Wartime rations

Wartime rations (per person per week); (from 'Yours' magazine, May 2004)

Meat	Is 2d worth (6p today)
Bacon and ham	4oz
Butter	2oz
Cheese	2oz
Sugar	8oz
Tea	2oz
Eggs	I per week, if available
Sweets	3 oz

Dinah Evans. Scarborough

Public catering

Rationing applied also to public catering. I helped to run a Scout and Guide Group canteen for the soldiers. The Group had to apply to the Ministry of Food for points for groceries and a small ration of butter, which were granted. We were able to provide the soldiers with tea, made in an urn in the kitchen, and cheese rolls. Sometimes we would have enough points to buy tins of 'Spam', a sandwich meat, and rolls of this kind were seized upon eagerly. We charged three ha'pence for these. Tea was a penny, as were the cheese rolls. We always made a profit.

Sheila Lacey. Dronfield

Rationing

Two ounces of butter did not last long and the margarine was 'cart-grease' type. Ration books were issued and we had to register with various shopkeepers. Lord Woolton, the Food Minister, introduced the 'Woolton Loaf' largely made up, we felt, of floor sweepings. Queues abounded even though we did not know what was on offer. Frequently the shutters were brought down just as you reached the counter.

Enid Edwards. Walton

Eking out the butter ration

I remember during the war, when food was rationed, my Mum would put our ration of two ounces of butter or margarine into a glass bowl, pour a pint of milk over it, then give me the bowl and a fork. I would whisk it for what seemed like hours, until we had a mixture of very light buttery substance. That two ounces and a pint of milk would increase our ration to about half a pound.

Graham Anthony. Chesterfield

Bananas!

Across the road in a field was an American searchlight. The first banana my sister and I ever saw came from the Americans because our Father had chickens and we got pigswill from the Americans. One day there was a piece of cardboard over the pig swill with a hand of bananas on the top. Something new to us and eaten with glee.

Peter Robson, Chesterfield

Raisins

Food rationing severely restricted our diet but the Ministry of Food tried to provide something extra at Christmas, perhaps an orange per ration book. One year – great excitement – we heard that there were to be raisins, those large moist raisins that contained pips. When my Mother brought home that week's groceries she solemnly showed us the raisins – all five of them! It was a very small pudding that year.

Daphne Isherwood. Tibshelf

The pig club

The village pig club was formed and the animals were kept at Mr Gregory's premises at 2 New Road (Holymoorside). The pigs were bought by a syndicate of villagers and the members were responsible for feeding on a rota of one day every two weeks. I used to help my Grandad when his turn came round. The members had half the pigs and the Government the other half when it was time for slaughter.

P's for Protection Potatoes afford;
O's for the Ounces of Energy stored;
T's for Tasty, and Vitamins rich in;
A's for the Art to be learnt in the Kitchen.
T's for Transport we need not demand;
O's for old England's Own Food from the Land;
E's for the Energy eaten by you;
S's for the Spuds which will carry us through!

Later in the war we had our own two pigs at Ashmore's farm on Loads Road. One day I arrived to see my Mother swaying backwards and forwards in the sty, clinging to the wall for support. One of the piglets was having a game by biting the bottom hem of her coat and shaking it. It was very strong and needed a bash with the brush to make it let go. Another time they escaped up the road but were caught before they could cause any trouble.

Frances Showell. Holymoorside

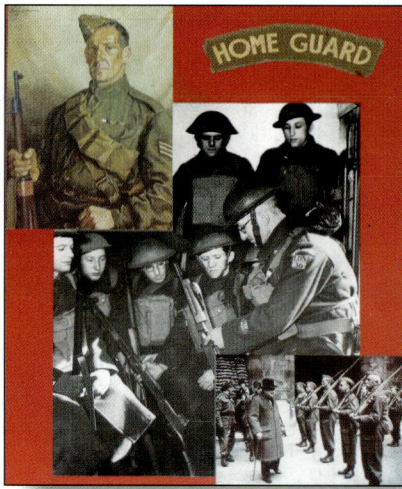

Home Guard poster

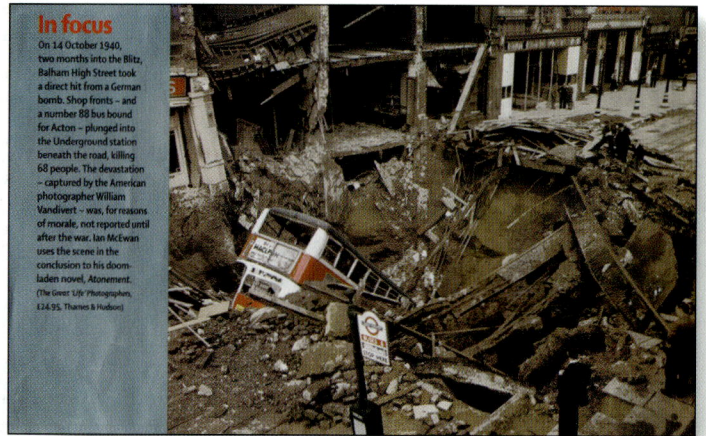

Bomb crater around a double decker bus

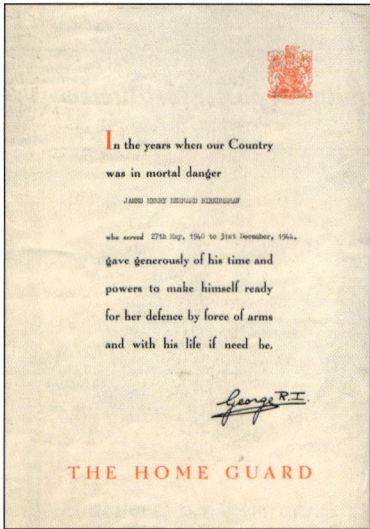

Letter from King George VI to the
Home Guard

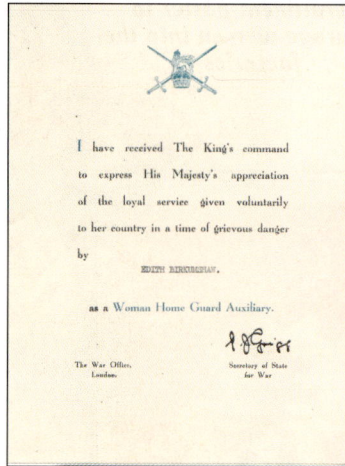

The King's appreciation

Warning to would-be looters

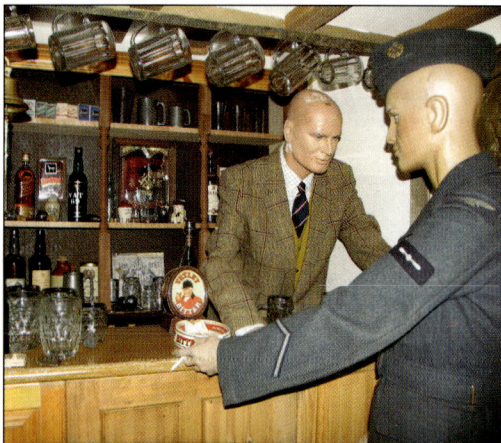

Museum tableaux
- the local

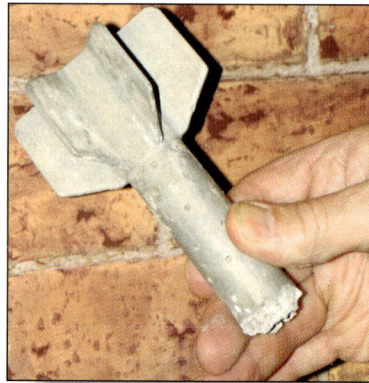

Tail fin of an incendiary bomb

ARP stirrup pump

Dried milk pwder

Queuing for food

Dried egg powder

Sweets worth one coupon

Mending kit

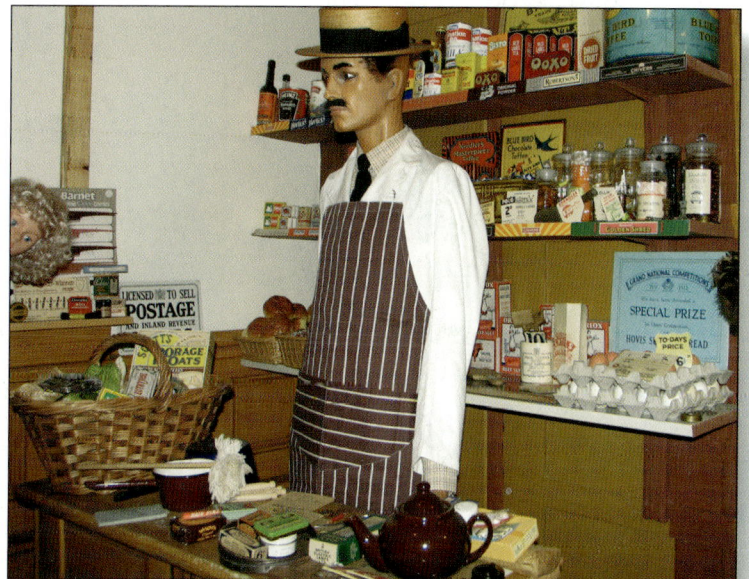

Museum tableau - the grocer

Clothing coupon book

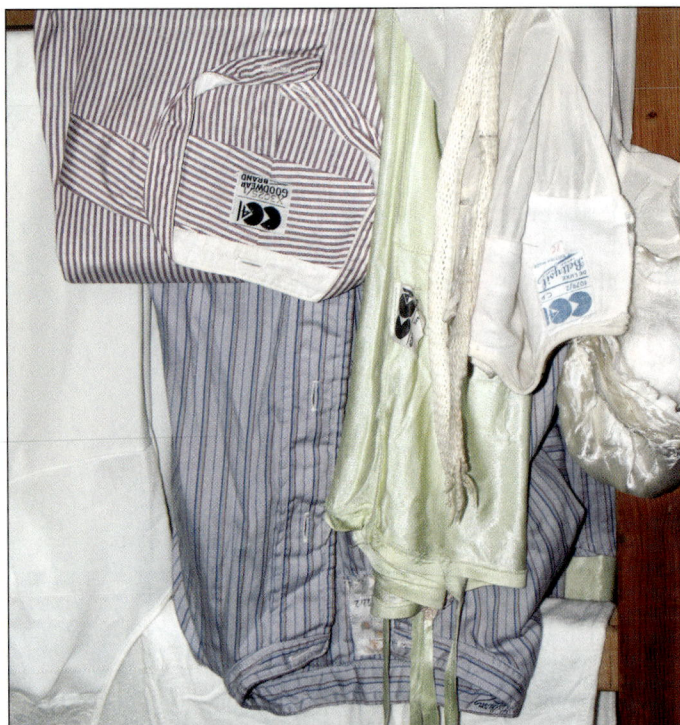

Utility clothing

D-Day poster

Poster - Make do and mend

Motor fuel ration book

Zoe Gail

Deanna Durbin

Stuart Hibberd

Football memorabilia

Frank Phillips

Music memorabilia

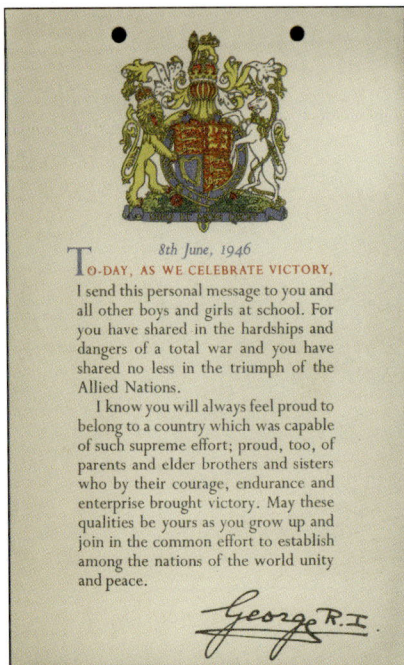

Letter from King George VI to all school children

Radio comediennes

Prisoner of war pack

Alvar Lidell

VE Day in Holymoorside

The corner shop

Our Father and Mother ran a corner grocery shop at the corner of Chester Street and consequently we were never short of food. A Sunday job was to clean the bacon slicer. Salt was sold in large blocks as paper packets were hard to obtain. The coupons from ration books had to be counted carefully each week and taken up to the Senior Food Officer. Next week's supplies depended on this being correct. Chip shops were very popular because these were extra to our rations though some said they used rotten potatoes. You could get a packet of batter for a penny.

Harry and Iris Husband. Walton

Difficult choice

November brought the Christmas fare to the local Cooperative store. Mother had to decide between a few bananas, a tin of tomatoes or a tin of fruit. Just the one selection, no more.

Barry Woodcock. Chesterfield

Half a dozen eggs

Fresh eggs were a much sought-after addition to austerity diet. Dad came home to say that he had put his name on a list of customers being compiled by a friend of a friend for the occasional half dozen eggs from his newly acquired poultry. Time passed with no eggs and Dad again met his friend who told him that everybody was having to wait as his friend only had one hen and that it hadn't come on to lay yet. Weeks later Dad came with the news that all orders were cancelled as the hen had turned out to be a cock.

We got our own half dozen pullets (all with pet names) that we kept at the bottom of the garden for the rest of the war. Dad's story lasted much longer.

Geoffrey Copley. Holymoorside

Feeling guilty

We kept ducks and chickens at home and had rations of 'balanced meal' for them. Corn was unobtainable except by farmers. Mother had been visiting a farmer friend and he had given her a very small bag of corn. On returning into the village she met our village policeman who stopped to talk to her. Afterwards she said she had felt so guilty having the corn in her bag, she felt sure he would know she was carrying it.

Frances Showell. Holymoorside

Sweets

Sweet ration time. Big decision time – do you eke out the sweets over a month? Or buy the lot and eat them at once? I used to eke them out, my Mother doled out sweets to my brother but my cousin scoffed the lot in one go!

Jean Birkumshaw. Holymoorside

WELFARE FOODS SERVICE

NATIONAL DRIED MILK

MODIFIED DRIED FULL CREAM MILK
THIS TIN CONTAINS THE EQUIVALENT
OF SEVEN (7) PINTS OF MILK
WITH VITAMIN D ADDED

CONTAINS NOT LESS THAN 280 I.U. OF VIT. D PER OZ.

ASK AT THE INFANT WELFARE CENTRE
FOR COD LIVER OIL COMPOUND
AND CONCENTRATED ORANGE JUICE.

PACKED UNDER GOVERNMENT CONTRACT FOR THE WELFARE FOODS SERVICE

National Dried Milk

Holymoorside Women's Institute

It was agreed that each member would bring one teaspoonful of tea for the 'Holymoorside blend'.

It was decided to form a nettle-picking party with a view to helping in the herb collecting and drying campaign.

The Rural District Council appealed for help in the organisation of a flag day for the Lord Mayor of London's National Air Raid Distress Fund.

It was proposed that a public meeting should be held in the Village Hall for the purpose of forming a Fruit Preservation Centre.

It was decided to form a party to collect blackberries for the Fruit Preservation Centre.

Satisfactory progress was reported from the Fruit Preservation Centre – 170lbs of jam have been made.

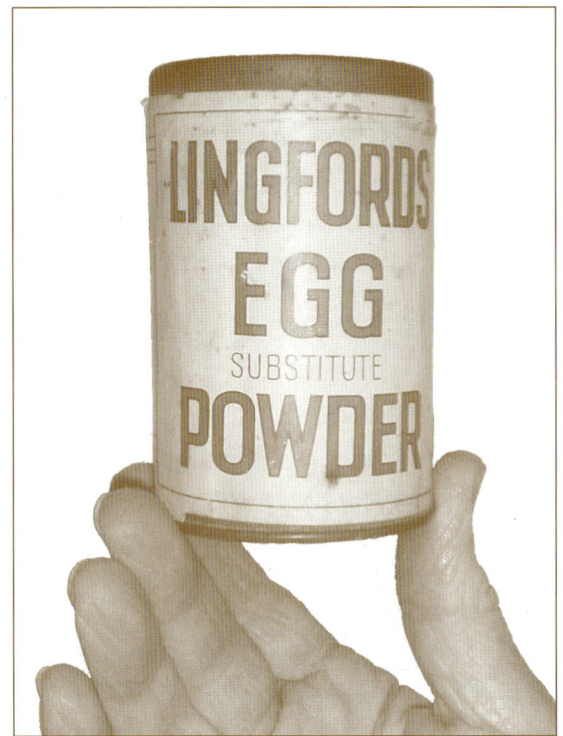

Dried egg powder

A talk was given on Post War Planning – a subject which must be kept in mind while we are winning the war.

A talk was given on meatless dishes. The recipes will be most useful as meatless days are a regular occurrence.

A letter was read from the Duchess of Devonshire appealing for help for the Prisoners of War scheme. It was decided to hold a concert.

Toys are to be collected from members for children evacuated from Malta and Gibraltar.

It was decided to distribute cod liver oil and fruit juice from the Village Hall at half-past-two on alternate Tuesdays.

Members agreed to gather rose hips.

Members agreed to take part in the opening procession for 'Salute the Soldiers' week.

It was decided to hold a dance in aid of the Friends of the Forces fund.

Members reported a shortage of children's shoes, woollen goods and sheets.

Extracts from the Minutes of the Holymoorside Women's Institute 1941-45

Fruit preservation

'To ensure that surplus produce should not go to waste the Government allocated sugar for the WI Fruit Preservation Scheme. Between 1940 and 1945 more than 5300 tons were preserved by members for the national food supply.'

WI Home and Country, September 2005

Austerity – make-do and mend

'Make-do and mend' was the order of the day. Clothing was rationed from June 1941 on a points system. Utility clothing and furniture were introduced to save materials. Men's trousers were made without turn-ups and women's skirts were short, plain and straight. Furniture was serviceable - there was little imported wood, and metal was needed for munitions. Materials were used and re-used, old clothes were darned and mended with needle and thread. Salvage, in the form of scrap materials, was collected for reprocessing. Aluminium household goods were sacrificed to make aircraft. Iron railings were removed from houses and parks to make ships and tanks. Wall tops with the stubs where the railings were removed can still be seen.

Make-do and mend

To keep warm in winter, when fuel was rationed, we knitted thick woollens. When the wool ran out we unpicked and unravelled old jumpers, washed and straightened the wool and knitted it into Fair Isle jumpers. My Mother and I joined a group to knit socks and scarvesfor the troops and small squares that we stitched together to make blankets for hospitals. Socks with holes in them could be darned or, if too far gone, made into mittens.

Dresses were unpicked. One adult dress could be made into frocks and blouses for children. Collars were turned to prolong the life of a shirt and the tails were made into cuffs. We patched trouser bottoms and jacket elbows.

We bathed in five inches of water and were recommended to paint a 5 inch watermark round the bath. We used the water for the first wash of our clothes.

We saved soap. 3½d a tablet may seem cheap by today's standards but even the final scraps were put into a small metal basket that we swished in the washing-up water for the dishes. We planted vegetables in small flower borders and kept hens to provide eggs, meat and bones to make stock for home grown vegetable soup. Everything was recycled, even the newspaper could be used in the loo. I still save wrapping paper, old bags and string.

Anon

Doing your bit

Everybody did their 'bit' towards the war effort. As a Girl Guide I was taught to knit balaclavas and thick double squares to hold the hot, flat irons. These were sold and we raised 9/7d (almost 50p) towards Churchill's appeal to help on the Russian front. Many young mothers went to work in the munitions factories, doing unusual jobs like welding and making aircraft frames.

Betty Holmes. Holymoorside

Village activities

People did what they could to live as normal a life as possible by helping one another. Khaki wool was provided for us to knit scarves for the soldiers. I often wondered if they wore them as the yarn was so rough and

"Do I mend?"

scratchy. In needlework classes at school, we brought socks and wool from home and learned how to darn them. Allotments were created in a field near our house and Mother took one to help to produce vegetables for us. It was all part of the "Make-do and Mend" campaign. Families had fathers, sons and daughters in the forces and some did not return. It was a sad, hard time.

Joan Baltare. Holymoorside

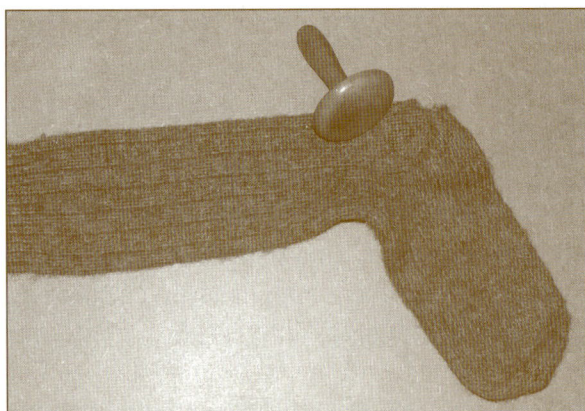
Sock with a hole and a darning mushroom

Clothes rationing

The rationing of clothes was announced in 1941. Each man, woman and child received 66 coupons a year. Even knitting wool and handkerchiefs needed coupons. A 3-piece suit for a man took 26 coupons; a woollen dress took 14. The nation was told not to waste anything and people had to improvise. Socks and stockings had to be darned, using a wooden mushroom; clothes and sheets were patched. Dresses were short, just below the knee, and without pleats. There were no double-breasted suits. Utility clothing was introduced in 1942 but the quality of the material was good and the blankets lasted for years. Children's shoes were also strong.

Skirts could be made from Father's old flannel trousers and a coat from two old blankets.

E. Mary Wardale. Holymoorside

Few pockets

Clothes were rationed and the number of pockets on men's suits was limited to save material. School blazers had only one pocket.

Mollie Lawson. Holymoorside

The 'squander bug'

I remember an adult model 'squander bug' being brought to school to urge the children to economise.

Peter Robson. Chesterfield

Deprivation?

I don't ever remember feeling deprived. My Mother saw to it that we were all well fed and clothed. My winter jumpers were 'Fair Isle' wool. My vests, liberty bodices and socks were 'Chilprufe', my shoes 'Startrite'. We went to Glossop for those having our feet checked on the x-ray machine.

Ella K. Neal. Dronfield

War-time Christmas

"Nighty-night. Sleep tight!" Grandma turned out the light at the bedroom door.

"Hope the doodle-bugs don't bite!" I answered.

But I didn't worry about the bombs that night. It was Christmas Eve and my Dad's long pit sock was tied on the end of my bed ready to be filled. But with what? There wasn't very much in the shops and even if you found anything, it was rationed. I knew Mam and Dad had been saving all their sweet coupons for me so there would be a bag of liquorice bits and another of fruit gums. A rather soft apple and a wrinkled pear, saved since the autumn, would fill the toe of the sock. But what else would there be? Mam had been cutting up an old red blanket; I knew she was making something for me, but I didn't want a blanket dress. I knew I wouldn't have any new toys because all the factories were too busy making tanks and bombs. But there was a shop in town called the Dolls' Hospital where old toys were mended and sold. Perhaps Dad had been there and found a surprise for me.

Suddenly I heard the air raid siren wailing. I sat up in the darkness and listened to the throb of a plane passing overhead.

Then Dad rushed in, lifted me out of bed, wrapped his overcoat round me and dashed down the pitch-black stairs.

"Into the pantry, all of you," he ordered.

As he spoke, there was a rush of wind, as if every window in the house was open, followed by a high-pitched whining. We fell flat down on the hearthrug, Mam pulling me under her. Then there was a loud bang that hurt my ears even though I was underneath. The house shivered and glass shattered into the back yard. From under Mam's arm I saw the coal fire go out as if it had been turned off. Then it lifted and fell back into the hearth.

"We must get into the shelter," said Mam.

"No, it's not safe out there," said Dad. "There's bricks and shrapnel falling. Get into the pantry – right under the stone slab."

The slab was a thick concrete shelf at the back of the pantry, where milk and meat were kept cool by a ventilator brick. I had often played dens there, but never with Mam and Grandma!

"Don't come out until the all-clear goes," said Dad. "Here's the torch. I'm off!" Dad was an air raid warden.

In the pantry it was pitch dark. "I'm cold, Mam," I wailed.

"Here, take this!" Mam clicked on the torch and passed me a newspaper parcel, tied with one of my old hair ribbons.

"What is it?" I asked.

"It's your Christmas present," she said. "You should wait until morning but I think you need it right now."

In the feeble torchlight I tore off the paper and pulled out something like a small red blanket. I held it up and discovered it had an arm – and another – and two legs. It was a siren suit!

"Oh, Mam, it's wonderful – thanks!" I'd been wanting a siren suit ever since I'd seen Winston Churchill in one, on the newsreels at the cinema.

I scrambled into my new siren suit. Mam had taken a long zipper from an old travel bag and sewn it in, all the way up the front.

Cosy and warm, I lay wrapped in Dad's overcoat, listening to the creaking timbers. I was even allowed to have a sip of Christmas port Grandma had found. I was happy under the stone slab with Mam and Grandma.

"Happy Christmas!" said Grandma.

And, oddly enough, it was.

Bette Paul. Higham

Dress alterations

After school I got a job doing alterations to dresses in the workshop of a large Sheffield store. My first job on getting to work was to light the fire that was needed to heat the irons. I had to polish the irons with soap and a cloth to keep them smooth. Openings in dresses had to be small to reduce the number of buttons and press studs needed. Cotton from unpicked hems had to be saved and used to sew up the new hem. Wool from worn out knitted items was used to knit and darn socks. We would use the lining out of a coat to make a skirt.

Ruby Wilkinson. Beighton

Operation 'Salvage'

It was a small cardboard disc with a safety pin on the back. On the discs were the various ranks of the British Army. For small amounts of salvage paper brought to the school, a pupil would receive a distinguished award of being a Private or even – a Lance Corporal. For larger amounts of newspaper, magazines and books, promotion to Sergeant and Staff Sergeant would be pinned on one's Fair Isle pullover.

One morning, the school was the recipient of some fifty or so large brown paper sacks. Four boys were soon elevated to the rank of Colonel and they made the fact well known to the rest of the school.

Later that day, a visit by the local Constabulary enquired why a huge deposit of cement powder had been found scattered at a nearby building development? Why had the sacks been found at the school?

At the court martial proceedings, in the office of the Headmistress, the three-foot high Colonels were stripped of their ranks.

Barry Woodcock. Chesterfield

Soap rationing

Soap was rationed in February 1942 to 3 ounces of toilet soap a month. Washing powders, such as Persil and Rinso were also rationed. Clothes were washed in a dolly tub once a week and the water was pressed out using a mangle. Underclothes were washed more frequently in a bucket. Hair was washed once a week.

Shaving soap and cream were not rationed but, like razor blades, were in short supply. People were asked to return toothpaste tubes to the chemist's shop – the metal was to be used for munitions.

The Ministry of Light and Power urged people to have a shallow bath of hot water. Domestic coal was restricted to 1 ton a month.

E. Mary Wardale. Holymoorside

Travel

Trains and buses were crowded. When our Grandmother was ill, Mother had to obtain permission to travel to Worcester to see her. Petrol was rationed but relatively few people had cars. Because Father gave lectures in army camps he had a petrol allowance, and on a couple of occasions managed to arrange his commitments so that he could take us as a family for a week's holiday in the Yorkshire countryside.

Dinah Evans. Scarborough

A journey by rail

In the middle of November 1940, Mum decided we should go to Liverpool to see Dad who was working there at the time. We set off from Euston station early in the morning and headed northwards expecting to reach Liverpool in five to six hours. The train was full of servicemen, most sleeping or playing cards. The train kept stopping, sometimes for ages, and we were completely off-course. There was no buffet car and so no food was to be had on the train. I did manage to dash out once when we stopped and get a couple of drinks but I nearly missed the train when it moved off again. It took sixteen hours to reach Liverpool. Later we heard that Coventry had been bombed heavily the night before.

Peter Rothwell. Chesterfield

A solution to petrol rationing

Travel by milk lorry

The milk lorry that came from the bottling centre in Sheffield to my Grandparents' and other local farms was allowed to carry the occasional passenger. My parents used this to visit me and, several times, I went the other way. It was dreadfully hot in the cab.

E. Mary Wardale. Holymoorside

Home to Chesterfield

When I was in the Women's Land Army I always managed to get home to Chesterfield for Christmas. I was issued with four railway passes a year. I would finish the day's work and catch the 8.30 p.m. train from Oxford. It passed straight through Chesterfield, arriving at Sheffield at midnight. The next train back to Chesterfield was at 6.30 a.m. The YMCA had bunk beds for threepence. If I came through Birmingham, I could get a bunk bed there. I once slept on a table in the ladies' waiting room at Nottingham.

Joyce Parsons. Old Whittingham

Lux Toilet Soap advertisement

School

For some, school was disrupted by evacuation. Those who were evacuated, often with their teachers, had to start in new schools shared with the existing pupils. Those that stayed at home may have found their school closed. Teachers were mostly women, the younger men having gone into the forces. Materials, particularly paper and books, were in very short supply. Life at school reflected what was happening outside and one just accepted gas mask and air raid practices - often as a welcome diversion. There was free milk and your gas mask was always with you. Waste could be brought from home, for school salvage drives and even waste food (and not much was wasted) was brought for the pig that many schools kept.

Village school

At the beginning of the war I was sent from Sheffield to live, first, on my Uncle's farm at Darley Dale where I attended a junior school. As evacuees were coming from the big cities we could only attend for half a day. Then, when it was realised that the war was not going to be over by Christmas, I went to my Grandparents' farm near Belper and attended the village school at Shottle. (It is now a private house with a plaque to say that it used to be a school. I visited recently and felt like a ghost returning.) In the early days of the war in 1940, a number of young children came to Shottle from deprived families in the East End of London. They didn't stay long as they were homesick.

We had a first class teacher, Miss Haywood, who taught the basic subjects extremely well, also knitting, crafts, doll making, puppets and art. She was the only teacher for a class of 5 to 14 year olds. The children walked up to two miles to school. In the one large room there were two stoves, one at each end and hot pipes. All the pupils were given 1/3 of a pint of milk a day and in the cold weather we put the bottles on the pipes to warm it. This was drunk before morning playtime.

There were two yards, with outside toilets. Our games had been played for generations – skipping games, ball games, singing games, such as the 'Jolly Miller' and the 'Farmer's in his Den', and 'In and out of the Window'.

We designed and painted posters for the 'war effort'. I got top marks for a poster depicting seagulls over the sea to represent the Air Force. It was to raise funds for our airmen's families. Before Christmas, we had an Open Day for parents and grandparents. Our paintings were put up on the walls and our sewing, knitting and embroideries were on display, with models made by the boys. We put on a play, either a Nativity Play (we dressed up as best we could) or a puppet play, with the papier-mâché puppets we had made, and we sang carols. The British Legion was always remembered and we brought money to school. Many could only afford a few pennies.

For Sports Day, my friend Myra and I used to practice the egg and spoon race, with a pot egg loaned by Grandma who kept hens, and the sack race using borrowed jute potato sacks.

E. Mary Wardale. Holymoorside

The best days of your life?

The bombing in London brought Tottenham Girls' High to our school. They came with their own teachers and had the schoolrooms half days while we had the other half. The teachers were billeted in the town and one stayed with us for most of the war. Half-day school lasted about a year and then most of the Tottenham girls went back to London. The rest were amalgamated into the school and we had proper lessons again. This was an unsettled time as being a Quaker School we had some young teachers who were conscientious objectors. They would teach for a term or so while waiting to go to prison. For a short time they were sent to work on the land, or to ambulance units or to be Bevin Boys in the mines. Eventually enough old or unfit teachers were found.

After Dunkirk, things became more serious. When the bombing of London started, air raid warnings were too frequent and upset lessons, so a master and two boys would go on to the roof and we would not go to the 'strong room' until they could see enemy planes.

The school had two rooms shored up with pit props that were supposed to be safe. Brick blast walls were built outside all the downstairs windows.

Mollie Lawson. Holymoorside

Sharing school

Children from the inner city were evacuated to the countryside. We shared our school building with one of the city schools - we went in the mornings and they in the afternoons (or vice versa). At first there was no school at all for our younger brother when he reached the age of five, so my sister and I used to try to teach him to read and write.

Dinah Evans. Scarborough

Lessons in the air-raid shelter

Our mining village had never been bombed but the Headmaster said that the school had to be prepared. So every Wednesday afternoon he walked along the corridors ringing the hand bell and we had to pretend there was an air raid. It was like fire drill is today but much more fun! As the bell clanged up and down the corridors we all grabbed our gas masks and filed neatly out in twos, across the playground and into the underground shelter. It wasn't really underground; it was an Anderson shelter, built of curved metal and covered with grass banks. But as you went into the blackness it felt like going under the earth. It smelt like it too, dark and damp. Half-blinded, we stumbled along wooden duck-boards down to the end of the long, arched shelter.

Ahead of us a teacher lit paraffin lamps, hung along the roof bars, and we looked for a place on the benches which ran down the sides of the shelter, right side for boys, left for girls. There was a lot of chattering and giggling and swapping of places but as soon as the Headmaster shut the door with a great clang, we were silent and still. We sat waiting for our orders.

"Gas masks ... OUT!" The Headmaster yelled at us, like a sergeant major at his troops.

We scrabbled in our little cardboard boxes, pulled out the gas mask and held the rubber straps ready for the next order:

"Gas masks ... ON!"

This was the difficult bit. The rubber straps got tangled in your hair and pulled it painfully. The metal snout often hit your nose. The celluloid visor always misted up so you could see even less in the flickering lamp light. And, worst of all, once you snapped the mask down under your chin, there was an awful moment when you felt as if you would never be able to breath again. And we were supposed to get into the mask in one minute flat! We always tried very hard because if we were on time we could have a barley sugar. Sweets were a great treat in those days of rationing.

After we had taken off our gas masks – in ten seconds – and sucked our sweets, it was time for the singing lesson. It was the only lesson we ever had in the shelter. That is what we did every Wednesday afternoon, after playtime. Then came the real thing.

You couldn't play hopscotch, skipping or 'tiggy' with a gas mask bumping on your chest, so we used to pile them on the steps at the school entrance. That Friday afternoon, when the sirens wailed out, the playground was full of rushing, shouting, laughing children. We didn't even hear the air-raid warning. It was only when the Headmaster came running amongst us clanging his bell that we fell silent and heard the stomach-churning noise of the siren.

We raced to the door of the air-raid shelter and tried to push our way in. A teacher had opened the door, ready to count us in. Some hope! We squeezed through, three or four at a time. And all the time the sirens wailed and the Headmaster's bell clanged. None of the lanterns were lit, so we scrambled for seats in the darkness, wriggling into any space we could find, shrieking and giggling as we landed on someone's knee. It was so exciting we never thought to be afraid.

As soon as the door was shut, and a few lanterns lit, the Headmaster went into his gas-mask drill. But most of the gas masks were outside on the steps! Luckily it was quite dark, so the few that had them made a great to-do of flapping them out and putting them on, and those without just did all the actions. It was so dark and I suppose the Headmaster was so worried about the raid that he didn't seem to notice.

Gas masks were off in record time when the all-clear sounded and we sat back to wait for our barley sugars. The Headmaster just stood looking along the lines of children's faces turned towards him. Like our gas masks, the sweet tin had been left behind in the rush. Some of the infants started to cry.

Later we heard there had been no raid that afternoon; it was a false alarm. Still, it had been more exciting than mental arithmetic. Somebody said we would get our barley sugars at playtime. But we didn't. We didn't even get a playtime!

Bette Paul. Higham

"Dig for Victory"

Dig for victory was on all the posters and my school, so that we could do our bit, obtained a small field at the side of the vicarage. The Vicar had lent it to us so that we could dig for victory. The field was partitioned off into small areas for us to plant vegetables. The plots were at the side of the vicarage orchard and the Vicar had given us permission to take home any windfalls. Joe Geeson, the strongest lad in our school, ran into the orchard saying "I'll get us some windfalls." Grabbing hold of one of the trees he started shaking it like mad. Unfortunately, the vicar's manservant was up the tree. There ended our free apples.

Graham Anthony. Chesterfield

When the Americans came

Things changed when the Americans came into the war and took over surrounding aerodromes. They took over the Grammar School, the pupils going to Newport Grammar nearby. They also took over two large houses where there had been senior girls' bedrooms and where Domestic Science had been taught. Domestic Science lessons ceased and girls went into the sanatorium when there was a scarlet fever epidemic. The school was closed as there were no sick quarters.

The baseball diamond for the American airmen was on our school field. The swimming bath was used for survival training. Men in parachute harnesses were suspended from the roof girders and dropped, or they jumped from the top board into the pool where they blew up their dinghy and paddled down the bath. They were allowed coke to heat the pool and we could use it between times.

Domestic help had almost disappeared, so we children had to help out. The boys shovelled coke for the school boilers; girls laid tables and helped in the laundry with ironing, using gas irons with a naked flame above the sole plate. The boarders cleaned the bedrooms and the day children the classrooms. Some mental patients were let out of institutions to help.

'A Jerry Christmas and a Jappy New Year' was the slogan and 'Have an American for Christmas'. We had two who came on Christmas Day bringing food.

Mollie Lawson. Holymoorside

Hay making and potato picking

We only had a four-week summer holiday from school. During the holiday, my pal and I helped with hay-making on a local farm. How we itched and our skin came up in lumps, most probably caused by insect bites and scratches from the hay. There was only Calamine lotion in those days to soothe the skin.

In October there was a two-week 'potato picking' holiday. We were expected to go to different farms for a half or a full day, to collect the potatoes as they were dug out by the horse drawn machine. It was a back-aching job. At lunchtime, we ate our sandwiches in the fields and drank water or cold tea from a bottle. The farm workers wore stout boots and sacks round their shoulders, as there were no waterproofs for them.

E. Mary Wardale. Holymoorside

Men's tricks

At the end of the war

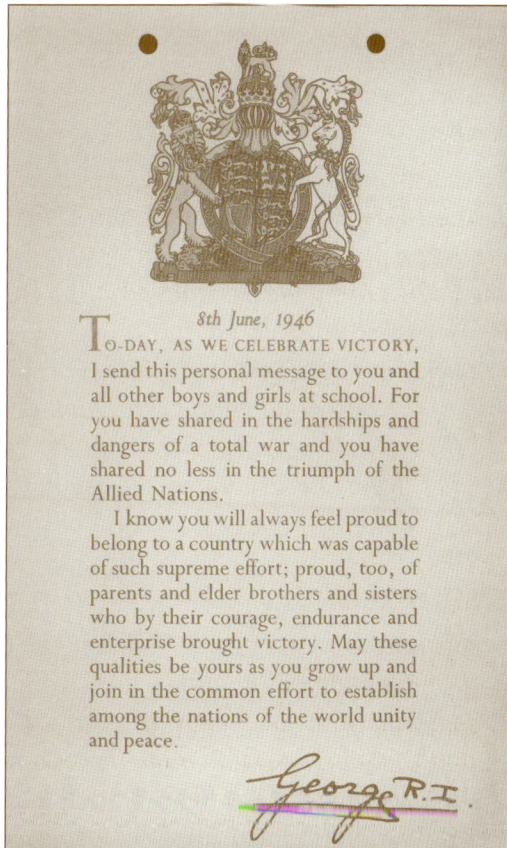

8th June, 1946

To-day, as we celebrate victory, I send this personal message to you and all other boys and girls at school. For you have shared in the hardships and dangers of a total war and you have shared no less in the triumph of the Allied Nations.

I know you will always feel proud to belong to a country which was capable of such supreme effort; proud, too, of parents and elder brothers and sisters who by their courage, endurance and enterprise brought victory. May these qualities be yours as you grow up and join in the common effort to establish among the nations of the world unity and peace.

George R.I.

Letter from King George VI to all school children

Dunkirk and after

The events of the war were reported to the Home Front (no doubt well censored) by wireless and newsreel film. Many a kitchen wall had a map, with flags on pins, to record the movements of the battlefronts. The nation rejoiced at successes and mourned setbacks. One of the most memorable actions, a major setback at the time but a stirring national effort and a chance to regroup, was the rescue of many Allied troops from the beaches at Dunkirk, where they had been forced to retreat after the fall of France. Here, the armed forces and civilians were in action side by side, crossing the Channel to bring the troops back.

Daily Sketch headline 31 May 1940

Retreat

During the spring of 1940 the news became full of battles, and then of retreats. We sang 'Run Rabbit Run' loudly but to no avail. As the German army swept through France and air raids took place, the full horror of war began to come home to us. France surrendered and the British army was stranded on the French coast. I remember the appeal on the wireless for small ships to go and rescue our men. Anyone with a small boat that could cross the channel was told where to report. They responded in droves. Every news bulletin was full of the desperate activity at Dunkirk. Pictures appeared of tired soldiers stepping out of fishing boats, rowing boats, holiday sailing boats. Many had suffered bombing on the beaches. Many never returned to England.

Sheila Lacey. Dronfield

Remember this!

I can remember Dad waking us in the night. It was June and dark outside. He lifted me to look out of the bedroom window at a dimly lit bus with people around it. He said, "I want you to remember this for the rest of your life, it will be part of your history." We were watching the soldiers coming back from Dunkirk. When the French surrendered in 1940, the British army was left to fight it's way back to England. Many of them got to the beaches at Dunkirk, some helped by local people. They were bombed and machine gunned from the air and still had to wade or swim out to the Navy ships off shore. The docks were

Soldiers return from Dunkirk

bombed and the beaches too shallow for them to sail in. As soon as this was known, hundreds of people set out in small boats from the south coast in an armada 'to bring the boys home'. As soon as the small boats, which were constantly being dive-bombed, got the men to the naval ships or larger pleasure boats, they left for England. About 350,000 men were rescued and taken to hospitals or ferried north away from the bombing. Many small towns received a quota and busloads of men were taken round the town with loud speakers asking residents to give them a bed. Some people actually refused to take 'dirty people' in and this caused resentment later. The look of exhaustion, the filthy uniforms and the smell of cordite, blood and dirty bodies is still clear to me.

Mother offered beds, baths and food and in the following days the billeted men walked to school with us on their way to the Ashgate Drill Hall. Many were sorted out fairly quickly and returned to their regiments, most coming back to say goodbye and thank you. Some stayed on until their unit was found and helped my Father dig out the air raid shelter.

Jean Birkumshaw. Holymoorside

Prisoners of war

During WW2, millions of people were taken prisoner and experienced treatment that ranged from excellent to barbaric. Many Italian and German prisoners in Britain and British prisoners in Western Europe were employed on farms to help with the severe shortage of farm labourers. Some settled and married local girls but most just wanted the war to end to return to their jobs and families.

Prisoners on the farm

Ploughing with horses

In 1944 I was still an evacuee and I was moved with my brothers to a farm near Coventry. The bombing was over and Dad wanted us nearer home. Farmers were desperately short of labour and Mr Phillips had taken on two Italian prisoners. They had been captured early in the war in the North African campaign. They had taken to farming like 'ducks to water' and were only too keen to pass on the skills to us boys. They taught us how to kill rabbits humanely with a single stroke of the hand – very useful as rabbits were part of our meat diet. At ploughing time we would rush home from school to watch Luigi and his two Shire horses manoeuvre the heavy plough before setting off on a new furrow. We wanted to get there in time for a ride home on the horses. We would help undo the harness to the plough and Luigi would give us a leg up while we grasped the large leather collar. The horses were so broad that our legs stood out like coat hangers and from our perch we could see over the hedgerows, as we listened to the jingle of the harness and the thump of heavy feet.

Luigi and Debiagio were both professional men and were longing for the war to end to return home to their families.

Adrian Marsden-Jones. Holymoorside

A threat

I remember my Mother recalling German prisoners of war from World War I working on her Grandparent's farm. At the end of the war one Prussian prisoner said to her Grandfather,

"We will come back and next time you will work for us." On hearing this my Father sat down at the piano and played and sang this song:

"We're going to hang out the washing on the Seigfried Line,

Have you any dirty washing Mother dear?

We're going to hang out the washing on the Seigfried Line,

If the Siegfried Line's still there.

Whether the weather is wet or fine

We'll hurry along without a care.

We're going to hang out the washing on the Siegfried Line

If the Siegfried Line's still there."

Peter Nightingale. Toronto

Bad feet

A work colleague, who had been a prisoner of war in the Low Countries, told me the following story. He had been put to work on a farm and one of his fellow prisoners suffered badly with painful corns, verrucas, blisters and calluses so much so that it was difficult to get his boots on. The old farmer told him to take off his boots and socks and to get on top of the manure heap. The manure had to be forked into carts for spreading on the fields. So the prisoner spent day after day in his bare feet on the manure. According to my colleague the man's feet were 'as smooth as a baby's bottom', by the time they had finished the job.

Geoffrey Copley. Holymoorside

The prisoners' bridge

The bridleway, between Chander Hill in Holymoorside and old Brampton was probably, at one time, the main route between the two places. At its southern end it is now called Westwick Lane. At one point the bridleway crosses a stream and, until the late 1940s, the crossing was by means of a ford. Towards the end of World War II a bridge was built to replace the ford. It seems that this was done using the labour of German prisoners of war from a prison camp located near Belper. The names of the prisoners are carved in the stone lintel of the bridge, with details of their camp – 'No. 58 Nr Belper Great Britain'. The prisoners worked at the flax factory near Belper and on local farms.

The inscription reads:

	R CHAPMAN	
	German POW	ERICH KONRAD
ER		
S. RAINS	Camp NR BELPER	HANS WOLF
		ARNOLD
	GREAT BRITAIN No 58	

The carving is legible and will remain as evidence of their presence here for years to come. The bridge is still in good condition and is in daily use by farm traffic.

Jean Morgan. Holymoorside

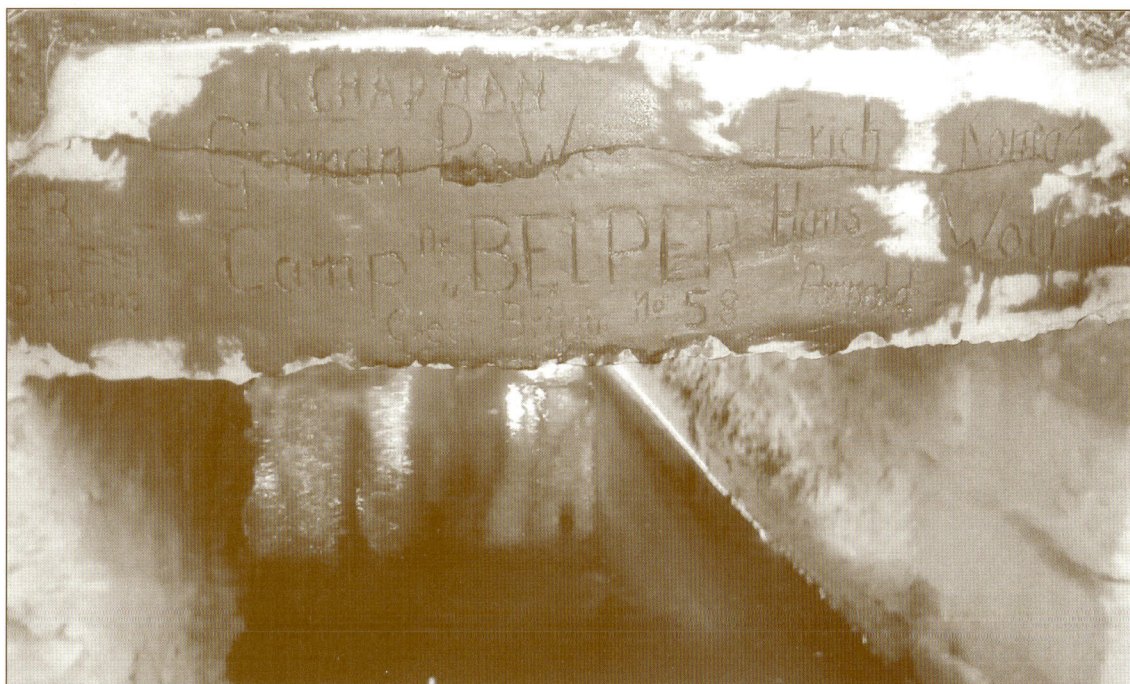

Lintel from the prisoners' bridge

Personal recollections

War was a time of 'bitter-sweet' memories with families separated and husbands and fathers away, and often in danger. Evacuated children formed life-long memories and were given glimpses of different ways of life that in some cases changed their lives. It was an impressionable age to leave home, often for the first time. The children that stayed at home remember everyday details of town and country life against the background of war.

Love

My husband was an orphan at ten years of age so he appreciated a home and family so much. He was in the navy and sent me this letter in 1943 after I had lost my first baby.

"The one thought behind my mind for months was that one day in the future I should meet you again. Just how to explain it, I don't know. It was something greater than the desire of man for his mate. There is only one satisfactory word for it – a small insignificant word with such a depth of meaning: LOVE!! A word that even the speaking of it raises bright gleams of hope through the dark skies of despair and sorrow.

But can anyone really explain love? We simply know that it is present and that we want to shout it out to the rooftops. Many people think they have it but their so-called fire of love turns to ashes of disappointment and sometimes, even hate. We however have indeed been granted God's greatest gift – perfect love." (Published in 'Writing of Love', Yorkshire Art Circus, 1996)

Joan Kirby. Walton

What do I remember about the war?

My brother, sister and I were orphans brought up in a Children's Home at Eastbourne. Other children were there, some because their parents could no longer care for them. There were about forty of us at a time. I was eight years old when war was declared.

We were issued with gas masks and had to practice putting them on and off over our mouths and noses in case of mustard gas attacks. (This had happened in the trenches in the First World War.)

I didn't stay long at this home and was sent with my brother on the train to a new home because it was considered too dangerous at Eastbourne. Bombing was expected. My sister was sent elsewhere.

Land Army girls worked in the fields at the back of the school looking after the growing of vegetables, so there was enough to eat.

All the windows were blacked out and if a chink of light was showing the ARP volunteers, who patrolled the streets at night, would shout 'PUT THAT LIGHT OUT'. We heard German bombers carrying out raids but never actually saw anything. It was still frightening.

My brother and I both had scabies while at this school and had to go to hospital to have purple paint put on our faces.

After a short while I was sent away to another school at Biggleswade. My brother went somewhere else. I never heard from him again.

I had quite a nice time at this Home. I remember watching tanks being transported to other parts of the country. It seemed exciting. I remember having to take newspaper down to the chip shop, where they would wrap our chips and we would sneak them into the

Home and upstairs to bed to eat under the bedclothes.

After a couple of years I moved again further away from the bombing to another Home. I can remember American servicemen staying in the area. Friends and I used to ask them for chewing gum but I got caught and was called out next morning in front of the school and caned. I felt very sorry for myself so played truant and went swimming in the river. I stayed there all day until the children came out of school. I had to go back to the Home because I had not had anything to eat all day.

We did not wear uniforms at school as they were considered to be too expensive. We were growing so quickly that clothes had to be handed down. We darned our own socks and had leather patches on the sleeves of our jumpers. Sometimes we were very hungry and would go around the neighbours asking if they had any food to spare. Sometimes they would give us cakes that were often old and mouldy. We also pinched apples from people's gardens, but they reported us and we were caned.

Life was sometimes hard, sometimes happy. We did not really know much about rationing. If the siren went for an expected air raid we went under the stairs or down the cellars.

By now the war was over in England and I was sent back to Eastbourne. It was strange to see barbed wire still in place on some beaches. They were out of bounds. Concrete gun towers were still in place – they are now classed as conservation buildings.

My brother and sister were not at the school and I have never seen them again. We did not have Identity Cards ourselves but the Homes kept them for us.

One day at school I had to go for an interview for the Merchant Navy. I passed and went to the Sea School at Tilbury. I was there for eight weeks. I had no money so spent any spare time wandering the streets or sitting on the beach. Occasionally a friend at sea school would give me a few pennies. All this changed when I joined the navy on a large liner that went to Australia.

Anon. Holymoorside

The war in Holymoorside

I was eleven when the war started and lived in Holymoorside. People were nervous due to the air of uncertainty. Our only sources of information were the radio and rumour. There were constant warnings about bombing and air raid shelters were being built, there was rationing (with warnings about hoarding), there was very little in the shops and above all there was the blackout which made people afraid to go out at night. It was particularly difficult for women on shift work in factories like Robinson's as there were no buses at night.

On Chander Hill there was only one outside tap for all the houses. On Monday morning, which was washday, we had to fill all the pots and buckets for Mother before going to school. In winter the first one out often had to thaw the tap. Otherwise village life continued much the same with farms and shops making life self-sufficient. There were lots of evacuees from London and Derby and there were many fights with the village boys to find their position in the hierarchy. Four of us went to dances in Clay Cross on two motorbikes, tied together with a scarf on the way back to save petrol! Sometimes Dad would carry a bale of hay in the back of his van, so that if stopped he could say that he was delivering it for essential war work! The village bobby, Mr Tyler, would sometimes stop you and hold a piece of blotting paper to the exhaust pipe. If this went black with soot he knew you were illegally using farm petrol. Although he wasn't above taking the odd bribe – the parcel left by the gate. Farmers were required to register their pigs so they kept moving them about to confuse him. There was a lot of swapping and barter going on of pigs' joints for rabbits, eggs and barrow loads of coal and the odd bribe, no doubt, helped to divert his attention. I remember one dark night he came cycling past with a sack over his shoulder, acknowledging me with just a curt "Good evening!" I can also remember black market butter that spurted water when you scraped a knife across it.

Mischief! We would climb on a shoulder to put a sod over the chimney pipe at the Bull after tying the pub doors together and then watched the confusion as those inside tried to escape the smoke!

Nothing was allowed to go to waste and we had bins outside for pigswill. The children were awarded badges starting at Private, Corporal, Sergeant right up to Colonel depending on the amount you collected.

Returning home from school we would all sit down to tea followed by games of draughts. Then we might listen to the radio, to ITMA or Lord Haw Haw. At 9 p.m. we rushed to bed to keep warm as there was no coal for the fire. The toilet was outside so, if necessary, we used the 'Jerry' under the bed. I well remember the freezing cold lino, hair sheets and wooden clogs for school. One-legged 'Cobbler Jack' used to stitch our leather footballs. In cold weather we would throw a bucket of water down the playground in the evening to make a slide for next day.

I once went to Manchester with five tons of hot-water bottles from Brampton Pottery. When we arrived there was a dense fog and I had to walk in front. There had been heavy bombing and many people were homeless and desperate to keep warm. They clamoured round the lorry even before we reached our destination.

On VE Day we had a grand procession with the band, tea in the gardens opposite 'Robin's Nest Cottages' and slow bicycle races.

Tom Tomlinson. Holymoorside

An adventure in the country

On returning from a ten-day camping holiday with the Boys' Brigade, on the Isle of Wight, I was told by my foster parents to prepare to be evacuated from south east London where we lived. The date was August 30, 1939 and it was the second time in just over a year that this had happened. This time Mr Chamberlain did not wave his little piece of paper and the evacuation of schoolchildren and mothers with babies was due to commence on Thursday 31 August.

I was 13 years old and overjoyed (though careful not to show it) at the thought of yet another holiday. On Friday 1 September we duly met at our school and marched the short distance to Ladywell railway station. We had labels around our necks, a gas mask in a little case over a shoulder and a small suitcase in which most of us had one clean set of underclothes, a shirt and one pair of pyjamas.

Many parents had come to the station and tears were shed by parents and pupils alike. This puzzled me as I could not understand how my schoolmates could possibly be unhappy in the face of an exciting adventure.

A train arrived and I can remember feeling vaguely disappointed. It was a very old train with a very small engine, not the sort of train that might whisk us across the country to Devonshire or even Wales. We had no idea where we were going, not even the teachers who accompanied us knew. In fact at that stage I am not even sure that the train driver knew the final destination. On boarding, we were told that if we had a special friend and would like to be billeted together we should tell whoever was in charge at our destination. They would do their best to meet with our wishes.

At this point I made what was almost certainly the most sensible decision of my 13 years.

Evacuees

The area in which I lived was one of the roughest in south east London and so were the boys that were my mates. I sensed that if I opted to be billeted with any of them I would never be out of trouble. Oddly I was also friendly with the class swot, a very reserved boy named Leon who appeared to have no other friends. We used to arrive at school very early and often chatted together until my pals showed up. He came from a better area and his parents even owned their own house! Quite middle class compared to most of us at our school. So I asked him if we could be billeted together and he agreed.

Eventually the train stopped We disembarked and saw the name of the station was Jarvis Brook. It meant nothing to us. On crossing to the exit via the bridge I shall never forget the disappointment I felt on seeing hundreds of grey, dismal looking roofs of small terraced houses. This was not what I expected in the countryside. Then, oh joy, down in the station yard were a number of motor coaches and it became apparent that this was not our final destination. After buns and lemonade we boarded the coaches and were taken a few miles to Rotherfield, a charming village about ten miles south of Tunbridge Wells.

It so happened that Leon was flushed and appeared to be running a temperature. It was decided that he should go straight to bed. The head-billeting officer, who was also head of the local WVS, was a maiden lady in her mid-sixties by the name of Miss White. When she enquired of the largely reluctant foster parents they all claimed that they had no bed ready. No way were they going to take on a sick little boy. So by another stroke of luck Miss White said she would take Leon and me too.

In due course Miss White (we never ever knew her Christian name) drove us about two miles out of the village in her car to her lovely house on top of a hill. Apart from a funeral, I had never even been in a private car, much less lived in a house with two bathrooms, five bedrooms, and a housekeeper, who lived in a cottage in the grounds with her husband the gardener/handy man. It all seemed too good to be true. Three days later it nearly came to an end for me when our form master, who I quite liked even though he had caned me more than once and certainly did not like me, found where I was billeted. He came to the house, apologised to Miss White for my presence, and said he would get me transferred to the village where my ruffian pals were. Thank goodness Miss White, who was strict but very fair, said she could not see a problem, as yet, and opted to keep me.

There followed the happiest few months it was possible to imagine. No school for over two weeks while a suitable large empty house was found and prepared. During this time Miss White used to take us out until we were quite familiar with the area. The local farmers all seemed to know her well and we could explore and play to our hearts content. The winter of 1939/40 was fairly severe and as the schoolhouse had no adequate heating we were frequently let off school for days at a time. We found an excellent toboggan in an outhouse and as long as we steered well there was a long downhill run to enjoy.

The spring of 1940 was pretty good and Miss White taught us a great deal about the wildlife and flowers. We got to love the countryside and both vowed we would live there forever. But one day in early June came the rude awakening. While eating my school lunch Miss White came in with a letter from my foster mother to say that I was to go home to London on the following day. I was 14 years and three months old and it was time I earned a wage. I was terribly sad but had to admit that I had not been learning much at school.

So it was back to south east London and my first job as an office boy (I hated it) at a tobacco company in Shoreditch. It did not last long as it was burnt to the ground on the very first weekend of the blitz.

My friend Leon stayed in Rotherfield until he was sixteen. We have kept in touch and he now lives in Tunbridge Wells. The last time I saw Miss White was in the mid-sixties. She was a very lucid and sprightly 92 year old, still living in the same house. She fell ill and died not too long after. The house looks smaller than I remember it as a thirteen year old and the hill not so high nor as steep, but it brings back the fondest of memories.

John Songhurst. Chesterfield

The war in North London

Pre-war events occurred which must have influenced the thinking of parents about the possible outbreak of war. There were two separate explosions at the local ordnance factory when the experimental explosive RDX went off prematurely, killing some workers and making a mess of the glass in the High Street and adjoining greenhouses. Then the noise of testing of Lee Enfield rifles and Bren guns was a background from my earliest childhood until well after World War II. Finally the open trenches in the local park, said to be for air raid shelters, were commonly believed to be for mass burials.

Most local children were evacuated on the outbreak of war. I was one of the few who remained. No official schooling was available as most teachers went with their pupils, and schools were closed.

After the phoney war, the piecemeal return of evacuees forced the reopening of local schools and for a few weeks there was some preparation for the all important 11+ exam, but not enough for my success. The Central School was for the narrow failures.

During 1940–45 certain events stick in my memory. The first mass air attack on London found me out walking with friends when anti-aircraft guns opened fire. We took shelter, unaware that a German plane had been shot down by the RAF and was coming screaming down at full power. It crashed less than half a mile away. Souvenir hunters were soon on the spot collecting bullets, pieces of metal and, allegedly, the seat of the dead pilot's trousers. That night, the London Docks could be seen burning.

In the winter of 1940 some part of London was bombed 72 nights in succession. We students spent much of the day and all night in the shelters. Our Anderson shelter was flooded when the water table rose and we spent the rest of the war sleeping in the house.

When the flying bombs (V-1s) first came, the only defence seemed to be a prayer that the engine would not cut out and plunge the bomb vertically down, but that it would carry on to some other target. One teacher at a local school was killed when she missed the cut out.

The authorities explained a succession of explosions in London as being due to 'exploding gas mains' but they were soon revealed as being caused by rockets (V-2s). George Kemish did not come to school one morning – a rocket had demolished his house, brought him down in the wreckage and killed his Mother. Another one was presumed to have fallen on a family walking home – presumed as no sign of them was ever found. Rockets travelled at 3000mph through the atmosphere.

For football matches we changed in school before walking to the nearby park. The park pavilion was reserved for air raid casualties.

We had a sound education taught by a mixture of women and retired men. Unlike the Grammar School we took the external Matriculation – get 5/5 subjects or get nothing. One of my friends got 4/5.

How did we entertain ourselves? It was not easy to move in the blackout, to travel any distance was impossible and rations were limited. The wireless was a help as the cutting off of a broadcast meant an imminent air raid! One thing I did like was the school dinner (costing 5d) with mince playing a big part.

Ken Medley. Holymoorside

Italy surrenders

My husband joined the Navy in January 1939 and served through the war to 1946. He was trained as a Radar Operator and went straight into war in September. In 1940 he was on the Curlew when it was sunk off Norway and afterwards he served in the Mediterranean. I still have the statement issued by Allied H.Q. that he received, as Radio Operator, and sent me following the Italian surrender.

"Italian Government has surrendered its armed forces unconditionally. Italians have been granted military armistice the time of which has been approved by the United States, Great Britain and the U.S.S.R. Italian Government has bound itself to abide by these terms without reservation. Armistice was signed by my representatives and representatives of Marshall Badoglio and it becomes effective this instant. Hostilities between armed forces of the United Nations and those of Italy cease at once."

Joan Kirby. Walton

"...and Dolly came too"

55

The Women's Land Army

The WLA was formed at the beginning of the war to recruit and train women to work on the land. First set up in WW1, the WLA was re-formed at the beginning of WW2 to anticipate the severe shortage of labour, as millions of men left the land for service in the armed forces or better paid jobs in factories. Women, with little or no agricultural experience and from all walks of life, were trained to do the jobs necessary to keep the farms operating. Home food production was essential during the blockade of British ports by U-boats.

Life as a Land Girl

Land Army uniform

My cousin and I joined the Oxfordshire WLA early in the war. We travelled from Chesterfield by train and were met at the station, then taken to a WLA Hostel in a large house near Woodstock. In our room we had a small wardrobe, a chest of drawers, which had to be shared, and a camp bed that had to be rolled up each morning and remade in the evening.

We had to launder our personal clothes by hand, wash our crockery, take turns with cleaning the sink and doing the ironing. Our uniform consisted of two shirts, one long-sleeved and one Aertex for work, a dark green pullover, corduroy breeches, socks, lace-up shoes, Wellingtons, a pork-pie hat, dungarees, three-quarter coat and a wax raincoat.

We arose at 7.00 a.m., had breakfast, packed our sandwiches and had to be ready for 7.45 for the forelady or supervisor to transport us to the farms in a 15cwt Hillman van which held 10 - with a struggle.

I was taken to a farm in a village with thatched cottages. We went threshing using a large machine with two of us on the rick feeding sheaves of corn into the machine and two girls removing the chaff and waste, a dusty job. There was a man in charge of the steam engine that drove the machine and another lifting the bags of corn on to the wagon.

We were trained in various duties - stooking corn, raking hay, baling and stacking straw, hedging, hoeing, potato sorting, mangel and swede picking, and we had some theory lectures.

Herdswoman

I went to another farm to learn milking. I was taught machine and hand milking, mucking out, feeding, washing and sterilising all the dairy equipment, and once a week stripping all the milking machines down, cleaning and putting them together again. I became a qualified milker and visited many farms as a relief during holidays for the usual herdsmen.

On one occasion Colin, the farmer's son, asked me to help him fasten up the bull. The bull broke out of the shed and knocked Colin down. I grabbed a pitchfork and ran to close the gate to keep the bull off the road. Colin had to be taken to hospital with a broken leg.

When milking, you put your head into the cow's side. They have bugs, similar to our head lice. I got them and my friend cut my hair short. I don't think they lived long. Once when I was milking, the cow turned its head and tore my trousers with its horn. I was teased, as I had to walk home with torn trousers. On one farm, I was the only girl and got teased a lot. I did the milking with the herdsman, a sneaky little man. I had to make sure there was always a cow or a milk churn between us, as he tried to pinch my bottom.

Mangel and swede picking

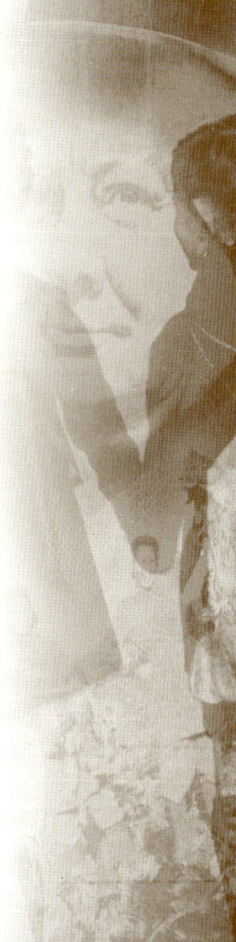

On another farm, I had to take the bull to the cow. I had a staff, a long pole with a hook on the end, for the bull's nose. It was a small bull shed and I was squashed against the wall. The bull wasn't interested in me but I think there should have been two of us as it could have been nasty. There was a cow with a bad sore on its leg and I was given the job of cleaning it. That stopped me wanting to be a vet.

One day, the farmer asked me if I knew what castrating pigs was about because that was what we were going to do. I said I knew vaguely. The pigs were for fattening for pork and bacon.

The cows stayed in the cowsheds in winter and if I had any spare time I would do field work which could be anything from potato sorting, mangel and sugar beet picking or hedging. The best jobs in winter were muck spreading and hedging which kept you warm – better than picking Brussels sprouts with frost on them. In the autumn I made silage. The cut grass was blown into the cart and then put into a large tank like a gasometer with layers of molasses, and trodden down.

Sometimes I helped with sheep. The sheep could get maggots and had to be dipped. As this was the law, a policeman had to be present at dipping time.

The hoeing team

I had three tricky episodes with horses. I was driving a horse and cart up a lane when I caught the gatepost. The horse started to bolt but luckily not near the road. Next, I was side raking the hay and couldn't stop the horse. I managed to turn it at the corner of the field and I kept on yelling until the farmer came to stop it. Then the next day, while doing the same job, the horse collapsed in the shafts. The lads said I had probably let it eat the hay and given it wind.

I went to one farm and opened the gate but closed it again quickly when about twenty large dogs came bounding up. The man shouted out "They won't hurt you" and they turned out to be Great Danes, Labradors and St Bernards – all big soft ones. I was put on sorting potatoes and we had to open the burrow (that is where the potatoes were stored covered in straw and mud). What a pong! We didn't find many good ones.

As a relief milker I was called to several farms on large estates. I did a lot of work at Ditchley Park where I worked with Italian prisoners of war. David Niven rode through the park on horseback. Some of the girls saw him and I was disappointed that I didn't.

I also worked in Blenheim Park, mostly potato picking. We went on parade on Rogation Sunday in front of the Duchess of Marlborough and had a service at Blaydon Church, where all the Churchills are buried.

"They looked that glamorous..."

I then went to another hostel near Chipping Norton. There were girls from all over the country. Some looked that glamorous and dainty you didn't think they would stay the course, but they did. It was the best of both worlds, working as a private land girl and enjoying the social life with the girls. There were two pubs, a village hall and a village shop. We generally got on well with the locals. They held socials and dances in the village hall and we had socials in the hostel and visiting speakers on health and beauty, VD and farming. On Saturday nights we would go dancing in Chipping Norton. A Yankie airman asked me to dance. Too late I realised he was a jitterbug dancer. I stood there while he danced. I met Harold, a young man from Hasland. We didn't meet again for four years until I returned to Derbyshire.

We also got invitations from the Americans at Brize Norton. They would fetch us in big trucks. They had lovely refreshments and they let us take home fruit cake and oranges. One of our girls married Earl, one of the Yanks, and another went out with one called Methuselah.

With the ploughing horses

We had a young farmer, Stan, who played the organ at the Methodist church. He used to come to fix our radiogram. He didn't mix socially with the girls until he met Betty, another Methodist. They have been married for fifty-four years.

The farmers and landowners were generally very kind to us. I worked as relief milker at Horley, near Banbury, for the Honourable Major Bailey. His mother, the Hon. Lady Bailey, paid for me to have a day off which gave me the opportunity to have a long weekend at home. She instructed the gardener to pack me a box of strawberries and other goodies.

Late in the war I made a request to learn to drive and permission was granted. Betty taught me. She had been a bus driver in Oxford. A man from the Agricultural Board tested me – I had to be safe to drive the girls about. I passed the test and later passed the national driving test when it was introduced in 1946. I was also asked to be Forewoman. My husband says I have never stopped being one.

Potato picking

When my Mother became ill I asked for a transfer back to Derbyshire and worked on a farm at Hasland. Harold, who I had not seen for four years since we were friends in Oxfordshire, was one of the first people I met. We married after the war.

I left the WLA when it closed down in 1950.

And a postscript from all those years ago

Two farmers, Fred and Gladys —

Fred said to Gladys: 'If you could produce eggs we could manage without chickens'.

Then he said: 'If you could produce milk we could manage without cows'.

Gladys said: 'If you were better in bed than the tractor driver we could manage without him!'

Joyce Parsons. Old Whittingham

Joyce

WOMEN'S LAND ARMY (ENGLAND & WALES).
RELEASE CERTIFICATE.

The Women's Land Army for England and Wales acknowledges with appreciation the services given by

Miss. J. Tipper,

who has been an enrolled member for the period from

15th January, 1944 to 23rd December, 1949.

and has this day been granted a willing release.

Date 20th December, 1949. WOMEN'S LAND ARMY

*WLA Release
Certificate*

EF/MP WOMEN'S LAND ARMY

Derbyshire

Tel. Matlock 522

Miss J. Tipper,
16 Eyre Street East,
Hasland,
Chesterfield.

County Committee

Imperial Chambers,
Dale Road,
Matlock.

9th February, 1944.

Dear Miss Tipper,

I am pleased to inform you that you will be required for work in the W.L.A. on Monday, February 21st. Arrangements have been made for you to go into training and subsequent employment with the Oxfordshire War Agricultural Executive Committee. The nature of the work will be general farming, including milking, tractor work and thatching. You will be billeted at the W.L.A. Hostel, Glympton Park, Glympton, Nr. Woodstock, Oxfordshire, with a number of other girls.

I enclose a railway warrant for your journey from Nottingham to Blenheim and Woodstock station. You should go by 'bus from Chesterfield to Nottingham and get there in time to catch the 1.32 p.m. train at the L.N.E.R. (Victoria) station. You will reach Oxford at 4.33 p.m. and should leave again from the G.W.R. station at 5.25 arriving at Kidlington at 5.35 p.m. where you will have to change trains. You should leave Kidlington at 5.38 and will arrive at Blenheim and

/over

WLA letter of appointment

By this personal message I wish to express to you

Miss. J. Tipper,

my appreciation of your loyal and devoted service as a member of the Women's Land Army from 15th January, 1944 to 23rd December, 1949. Your unsparing efforts at a time when the victory of our cause depended on the utmost use of the resources of our land have earned for you the country's gratitude.

Elizabeth R

A personal message from the Queen

Industry

Industry was directed to the manufacture of munitions and the support of the war effort. Some occupations were reserved as essential to the running of the country and to the production of armaments and coal. A consequence of so many men being away was that more women went into industry. This was a lasting legacy of the war. In Chesterfield, a town of heavy industry, many components such as airframes, landing barges, gun barrels, ammunition casings and bandages and medical products for the military hospitals were manufactured.

Local industry

The factories in Chesterfield had been changed over to munitions work. Sheepbridge made munitions and airframes, Tube Works made gun barrels, and bomb and shell casings, and Markhams made invasion barges and one-man submarines.

There were several clay pits along Harewood Road where they dug out white 'gannister' clay that was used to line factory furnaces. This was a major contribution to the war effort.

When I was fourteen I started work at Ploughwright as apprentice fitter installing machinery down the pits. I earned 14/9d a week. After paying Mum for board this left me 2/9d to spend. A dance cost 1/- and the bus fare 6d return!

Tom Tomlinson. Holymoorside

'Careless talk costs lives'

My Father was a turner at the Tube Works in Chesterfield. From the beginning of the war I was told not to speak to anyone about where he worked or what he did. The slogan 'Careless talk costs lives' was the order of the day. I used to ask "Is Dad at work or is he in bed?" He worked a 12-13 hour day so I rarely saw him.

Frances Showell. Holymoorside

Mining or metalworking

When the family settled in Holymoorside the village policeman told my Dad that he must go to see a man in Chesterfield who would tell him what to do for the war effort. He had to choose to be a coal miner or go away to do highly skilled metal work as he had been apprenticed to a blacksmith in his teens. He and my Mother were afraid of injury in the mines as he was a musician and his hands were very important to him. So he was sent to Birmingham to train to make machine parts. Then he went to Redditch where he worked for the Birmingham Small Arms Company. He could not come home often and we saw him only Saturday afternoons and Sunday mornings maybe three or four times a year. Many children in the village didn't see their fathers at all for many years.

Peter Nightingale. Toronto

Conscription

I worked for Robinsons in Chesterfield in the Cotton Wool Department. Locally we were referred to as Robinson's Angels. We were not allowed to volunteer but we could be conscripted to serve in the NAAFI, the Forces, nursing, munitions factories or the Women's Land Army. I was conscripted at the beginning of the war and chose the WLA. I had helped on a friend's farm and my cousin was already in the WLA. I served until 1950.

Joyce Parsons. Old Whittington

Industrial radiography

I was in Industrial Radiography during the war, a reserved occupation. Radiography enabled us to X-ray several inches of steel. Big steel castings for armour and turbine parts needed many weeks of machining. If defects or 'blow holes' were then found in the metal all that work would have been wasted.

We used radium salts that give off radiation with a 'half-life' of many years. We worked in the caves under Nottingham Castle and had to have a monthly blood test in the City Hospital. If your white blood cell count dropped below 5000, due to radiation exposure, it was considered dangerous. Mine once dropped to 4500 but they kept me on. I survived!

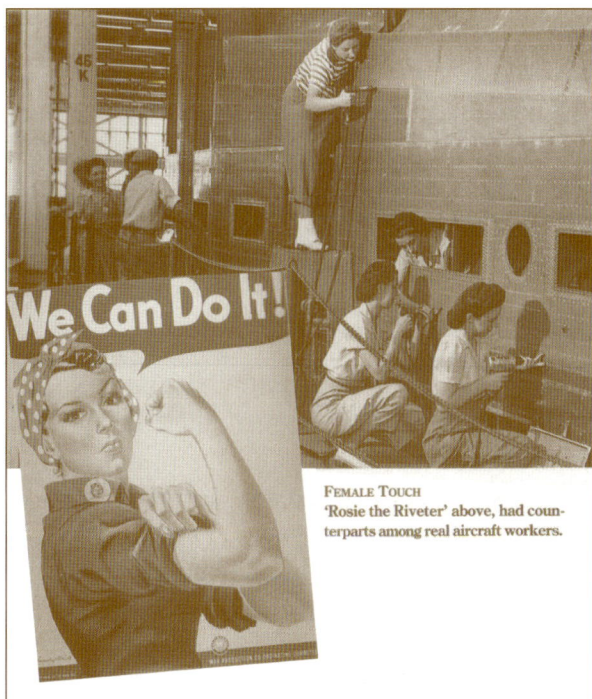

Recruitment posters

FEMALE TOUCH
'Rosie the Riveter' above, had counterparts among real aircraft workers.

We also X-rayed unexploded bombs to see if the fuses were booby-trapped and the first 'flying bombs' that crashed without exploding.

Eric Dove. Holymoorside

Crane driver

My Mother, at only 5' 3'', drove a forty-ton overhead crane at the Chesterfield Tube Works. The crane travelled the length of the huge factory carrying, overhead, the white-hot shell cases from the hot hydraulic press to the cold press where they were cooled. Pay day was Friday afternoon and if Mam was on nightshift she would go in specially to collect it, often taking me, an eight year old with her, crossing the deafening factory floor where all this war effort was taking place.

Dorothy Marsden-Jones. Holymoorside

Where can it have gone?

I worked for a company that during the war manufactured tubes for submarine periscopes. These were long and precision-turned on huge lathes. There was great consternation one day when it was realised that one of the tubes had disappeared. As this was a very high-security, high-secrecy factory, senior naval officers and men from the Ministry came immediately to investigate. It was impossible to see how the enemy could have got one of the long tubes over the wall and out of the factory. Despite intensive investigation the matter remained a mystery.

It was many years after the war that a senior engineer came to his retirement and explained what had happened. As a young machinist he had been working a long, night shift turning a periscope tube. To his horror he found that he had taken-off too much metal. Afraid to admit this he spent the rest of the night turning the whole tube down to metal turnings. These he had distributed in small amounts in all the waste bins in the factory.

Geoffrey Copley. Holymoorside

A new product

One day I was walking up Chander Hill in Holymoorside and saw the hedgerow covered in strips of aluminium foil glistening in the sunlight. We had no idea at the time, but discovered much later that it was called 'Windows' and had been tested to see if it could disrupt radar detection. Apparently it was used to good effect in the early days of bombing over Germany and must have saved many lives by confusing the German fighters.

Betty Holmes. Holymoorside

Women in industry

My Father was seconded by Winston Churchill to help in the mammoth task of creating and mobilising a workforce for the ordnance factories. With slogans such as 'COME INTO THE FACTORIES' there was a huge response from housewives throughout the country and by 1943, 90 percent of single women and 80 per cent of married women were 'doing their bit' working in munitions factories, civil defence, nursing, transport and key occupations to relieve men for the armed forces. This mobilisation of a determined workforce enabled the country to maintain production despite the bombing. Even throughout the Battle of Britain, despite heavy losses, fighter production was maintained and the number of aircraft never became a factor in the battle.

Adrian Marsden-Jones. Holymoorside

Machine tool operator

After the bombing of Sheffield, I lost my job in a dress workshop because the premises had been damaged. I went to work in a factory where I helped to make handles for hacksaws. It was heavy, noisy work and the smell of whale oil used to lubricate the machines upset me and made my hands sore. I learnt to use different machines for cutting, stamping and drilling the steel - perhaps because I wasn't good at any of them. I had to use two drills at once to speed up the number of parts made. It wasn't until 1946 that I was allowed to go back into dress alterations.

Ruby Wilkinson. Beighton

Entertainment

Bombing, the blackout and petrol rationing meant that much of wartime entertainment was in the home. The radio was a lifeline to news and comedy. The most popular comedy programme was Tommy Handley's ITMA (It's That Man Again) with characters still well remembered – Mrs Mopp, Colonel Chinstrap and Funf, the German spy. Children's Hour at 5 o'clock, with Uncle Mac, was a must for many. The recognition of the morale-raising role of entertainment was reflected in the formation of ENSA, the Entertainment National Services Association, in the first month of the war to enable stars to perform at home and at the war front for the fighting forces. Theatres remained open throughout the bombing. Workers' Playtime was broadcast in all factories. Glen Miller was the most popular dance bandleader and Chatanooga Choo Choo won the first-ever golden disc. Films, such as Gone With the Wind, have remained box office favourites and wartime songs still bring back memories.

Saturday cinema

Our entertainment was twice a week at the Odeon (now the Winding Wheel). It was always packed with kids. It cost two pence and you had your ticket stamped with a star. Ten stamps and you got a free show. Before the film we would always sing:

'Every Saturday morning where do we all go?
Stealing into mischief, oh dear no!
We go to the pictures where we sing this song
Every Saturday morning at the Odeon.'

Harry and Iris Husband. Walton

Country pursuits

While living on my grandparents' farm during the war we played as much as possible in the fields. We looked for wild flowers, walked through woods, particularly at bluebell time, climbed trees, made 'acorn' men and looked for birds' feathers and even skulls and bones. We made bows out of hazel branches and arrows from elderberry. They were not very satisfactory so I was thrilled when I received a bow and arrows for Christmas. We dammed the stream and made clay figures out of the wet clay. On wet days we sat in Granny's summerhouse and played games or read. In the autumn we looked for blackberries hanging over the walls and hedges. My friend's father owned a large farm nearby and we would play hide and seek in the cowsheds and hay barns, and climb the hay stacks. We had bread and honey for tea, fresh tomatoes straight from the greenhouse and milk fresh from the cow. In the winter of 1940 there was deep, deep snow, marvellous for children but dreadful for grown-ups. We sledged down the fields and tried to make igloos, but the roof always fell in.

E. Mary Wardale. Holymoorside

The Guides

We had Girl Guides, the Junior Choir, Sunday school anniversaries and picnics. We made soft toys out of old material, we picked blackberries for jelly and jam, rose hips for syrup and foxglove leaves to be sent for processing to extract digitalis. We had 'war efforts' to buy a Spitfire and parades. Later I used to help the Land Girl at Bage Hill farm to deliver the milk with the pony and milk float. There were no bottles just a large can filled repeatedly from a large churn. The milk was ladled into jugs and bowls that the housewives brought to the door to be filled using a measure hung on the inside rim of the can.

Frances Showell. Holymoorside

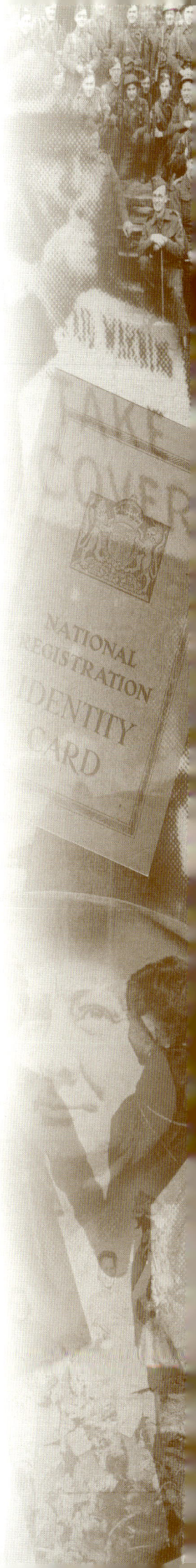

A visit to the theatre

During evacuation to Wales I saw the 'Old Vic' Company in Macbeth. I still have the programme signed by Sybil Thorndyke and James Casson. Tyrone Guthrie directed the play. Their tour was made possible by the Council for the Encouragement of Music and the Arts, a body set up to maintain the highest standards in the national arts at a time when they were most threatened.

Joyce Smith. Wingerworth

Parachutes

We made parachutes from a handkerchief, four pieces of string and a stone. Whether they worked or not depended on how you wrapped the hanky and wound the string and stone around it. Even if the strings unwound, the hanky didn't always open, like a mushroom, but just came straight down, like an arrow – it's called a Roman candle. I had a friend who said he was going to get a real parachute. His brother who was in the RAF knew someone who worked as a parachute packer and if the material was torn or frayed they could take it home. We were going to make a parachute from a circle of silk with eight strings. But it did depend on there being enough material left over after a wedding dress had been made for his sister.

John Pratt. Holymoorside

Holidays at home

There were no holidays at the seaside so 'Holidays at Home' were organised in Queen's Park. There were displays by the AFS (Auxillary Fire Service), the LDV (Local Defence Volunteers referred to by the variety comedians as 'Look, Duck and Vanish'). They later became the Home Guard and other groups. There were athletics for the children and cricket matches. One year to everyone's amazement the US Army played a game of baseball on the cricket pitch ('Good God!' George, a Derbyshire supporter, was heard to say.) There were Dig for Victory food shows and the paratroops gave gymnastic displays. Their training camp was at Hardwick Hall and they 'played' quite boisterously in Chesterfield. Revellers were often found in the static water tanks built in odd corners of the town in case of firebombs.

Jean Birkumshaw. Holymoorside

What on earth is it?

Returning home one very dark night in the blackout I passed under the theatre awnings where people queued for the cheap seats. Feeling my way along the cold wall I suddenly sensed there was something in front of me. Tentatively reaching out I felt a soft leathery texture and looking up I saw two luminous spots. What was happening? Surely they hadn't built a wall across the pavement. Then the penny dropped. There had been a circus at the theatre and I was feeling the side of the elephant! The two spots were the eyes of the Indian Mahout riding it back to its stables.

Eric Dove. Holymoorside

Our scooter

There were very few toys during the war. It was a red-letter day when my Father got a new wheel for our broken scooter. Good fortune shared with all the children in the road. We lived in a cul-de-sac and all the children lined up and took turns on the scooter to the bottom of the road and back again – then to the end of the line to wait for your next turn, no arguments, no squabbles.

Margaret Copley. Holymoorside

The war is over

Occasionally I got the opportunity to go to a West End show or cinema. Tommy Trinder, Ted Ray, many pre-war stars were performing despite the raids. I can remember going to see the Royal Canadian Navy Show, all performed by serving sailors. It was tremendous. Then back home on the Tube through all the stations by then filling with people settling in for the night to shelter.

I went to see a film. Halfway through, the lights came on and the manager came on stage and said, "Ladies and gentlemen, it has just been announced that Germany has agreed to accept unconditional terms of surrender. The war is over!" It was 7 May 1945. I can't remember whether they finished the film or not.

Peter Rothwell, Chesterfield

News and variety

The Readers on the BBC 9 o'clock News were household names, Alvar Liddell, Frank Phillips, Stuart Hibberd and others. They announced their names to reduce the possibility of the News being used by the enemy for propaganda.

Wireless and stage entertainers were legion: Tommy Handley, Arthur Askey, Bebe Daniels, Ben Lyon and Vic Oliver, Jack Warner and his sisters Elsie and Doris Waters (Gert and Daisy), Sam Costa, Jack Train, Vera Lynn, Anne Shelton, Tessie O'Shea, Gracie Fields, George Formby and many, many more helped to raise morale throughout and after the war.

Bless 'em all

I remember singing, at the tops of our voices, in the changing rooms at the baths, where the acoustics made it operatic:

> 'Bless 'em all, bless 'em all,
> The long and the short and the tall,
> Bless all the Sergeants and WOIs,
> Bless all the Corporals and their blinkin' sons.
> For we're saying 'Good-bye' to them all,
> As back to their billets they crawl,
> You'll get no promotion this side of the ocean,
> So cheer up my lads – Bless 'em all'.

It's funny how the words stick after all these years.

Anon

Popular songs

The songs of the time can still bring a lump to the throat -

Remember Vera Lynn?

'We'll meet again'
We'll meet again don't know where, don't know when,
But I know we'll meet again some sunny day.
Keep smilin' through just like you always do
'Til the blue skies drive the dark clouds far away.
So will you please say hello to the folks that I know
Tell them I won't be long...

'White Cliffs of Dover'
There'll be blue birds over the White Cliffs of Dover
Tomorrow, just you wait and see.
There'll be love and laughter and peace ever after,
Tomorrow, when the world is free.

And 'Lilli Marlene', popular with friend and foe alike

Underneath the lantern by the barrack gate
Darling I remember the way you used to wait,
'Twas there that you whispered tenderly,
That you loved me, you'd always be,
My Lilli of the lamplight
My own Lilli Marlene.

Vera Lynn

Football

At the commencement of war the Football Association cancelled all fixtures and there was no more League football until the war was over. Many of the league professionals and supporters were drafted into the forces, large crowds were considered to be unsafe in the event of bombing and travel was restricted by the shortage of fuel.

The 1939 – 40 season had just started and the last results and league tables show Chesterfield in the Second Division (now designated the Championship) alongside, for example, Newcastle United and Tottenham. Sheffield United were second in the First Division (now the Premiership) and had just beaten Leeds United. The old Third Divisions, North and South, remained for a long time after the war and were eventually merged into the present Leagues Two and Three. (Note the latest development in razor blades.)

Results, scorers, tables immediately pre-war

VE and VJ celebrations

Germany acknowledged defeat in the early hours of May 7, 1945. Hitler had committed suicide in his bunker in Berlin a week earlier. Winston Churchill and the new American Premier, Harry S. Truman agreed that the following day, May 8, should be celebrated as Victory in Europe (VE) Day. As with the outbreak of war, most British families heard the news on their radio. That night the streetlights were switched on for the first time since the start of the war and street parties took place all over the country despite the continuing austerity. The British election on July 5 saw the replacement of Prime Minister Churchill by Clement Attlee. The war against Japan continued until August and was comprehensively ended by the dropping of atomic bombs on Hiroshima and Nagasaki. Japan surrendered on August 14, 1945.

End of War in Europe
"Cease Fire" sounded midnight Tuesday
The King's tribute to his peoples

The Derbyshire Times, Friday, May 11, 1945

Clippings

VE Day was Tuesday, May 8, 1945. Flags and bunting appeared like magic and private houses and business premises were decorated. Throughout Derbyshire most of the big industrial concerns closed down except for limited staff and there were festivities in towns, villages and hamlets. A relaxation of the licensing regulations had been granted everywhere.

In Chesterfield when darkness began to fall there were scenes of revelry and thousands of people gathered in the Market Square, High Street, West Bars, and in front of the Town Hall. From loud speakers on the Market Hall came patriotic airs and there was community singing. Soldiers, civilians and girls danced in the Market Square. The Parish Church and the Town Hall were brilliantly floodlit and coloured lights were suspended the full length of the gardens leading down to West Bars

VE Day celebrations

and another lavish display of lights on the Market Hall. One got a good impression of what peacetime lighting looks like after nearly six years of blackout.

The Derbyshire Times. Friday, May 11, 1945

Street party

On Milton Crescent we had a street party to celebrate VE Day. Out came the paper chains, prized from before the war. It was decided to have red, white and blue blancmange. There was much discussion on how to get the colours. Mam had to make the blue one and she

VE Day street party

couldn't decide whether to use blue ink or a 'dolly blue' bag (used to whiten the washing). I think she decided on the ink, as did the person making the red blancmange.

After the tea, the children were all lined up in a crocodile to walk about three miles to the Hasland cinema. I could only watch the celebrations from my bedroom window as I had a bad case of impetigo. I had previously had scabies and was treated, as an outpatient, at Penmore Hospital. We were stripped down, scrubbed, painted all over with something like white distemper and then individual spots were painted with gentian violet. We were particularly distressed to appear in public with purple spots on our faces. However we escaped the ignominy suffered by some of our friends who had their heads shaved because they had ringworm.

Dorothy Marsden-Jones. Holymoorside

Cakes and jellies

We had a street party at the end of the war in the circle at the end of our cul-de-sac. There was a long table set out with cakes, jellies and whatever else could be gathered together in those days of continued austerity. All the children tucked in watched by our Mums and Dads. I remember being upset when a photograph was taken and another child's head was in my way.

Margaret Copley. Holymoorside

Near the end

VE Day saw a huge bonfire of railway sleepers near the local football field on which we had kicked a muslin flour bag, stuffed with rags, to destruction. The field had an unusual name – 'The Blue Fly'. At one time it had been the rubbish tip for the village and had attracted huge swarms of flies. The local licensee gave every child a threepenny piece. A lady on our street was upset and crying, her son had been killed by a sniper's bullet in

VE Day bonfire

the final hours of the war. Some families mourned the loss of their loved ones whilst others celebrated the return of their husbands and sons in new 'demob' suits. Mother went shopping with the ration books as she would continue to do for years. Our gas masks lay dormant in the wardrobe. I never did have one of the Mickey Mouse ones!

Barry Woodcock. Chesterfield

The end of the war

I remember May 1945 and the end of the war. I was seven and staying with my Grandmother who had been able to return to her home at the seaside. We were absolutely dancing around.

No more bombs, deaths, blackouts and we saw it as a brave new world more or less the following day.

Ruth Robson. Chesterfield

Memories

So there were good memories as well as bad ones and we were more fortunate than many – no close friends or relatives lost their lives, and my sister and I were allowed to continue our studies at University and College when we left school. Shortages of food, clothing, fuel and building materials lasted well after the end of the war, but at least we were able to abandon the blackout and switch on the lights. I marvel now at how my parents, and particularly my Mother, often alone at home with a young family, coped with those years.

Dinah Evans. Scarborough

Memorabilia

There were many parties and I was fascinated with the collections of memorabilia as soldiers, sailors and airmen returned to 'civvy-street'. Tins full of badges, buttons, shrapnel etc. We also had a wedding to celebrate on our street between a soldier and his Maltese girlfriend who had come back with him to England.

John Cuttriss. Newbold

VE Day celebrations

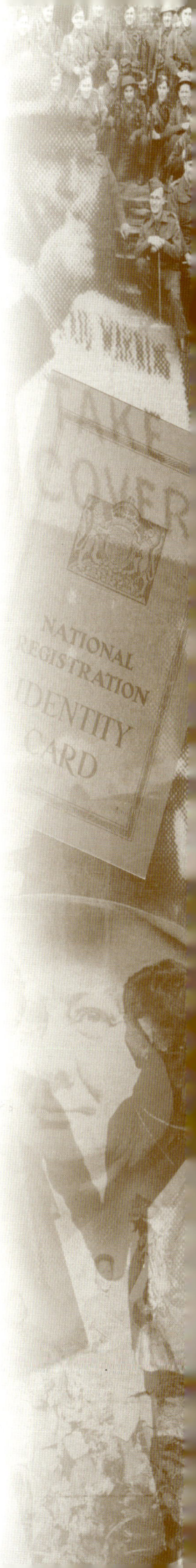

VJ Day

Mother had a sister living at Islington so VJ Day saw a visit to the bomb-scarred capital. We joined the celebrations outside Buckingham Palace. The size of the crowd dwarfed me but a Guardsman lifted me on his shoulders so that the Royal balcony and celebrities were in full view.

Barry Woodcock. Chesterfield

The very end

Attlee, at midnight, gives news that it is all over

PEACE ON EARTH

JAPS REPLY: WE HAVE THE HONOUR TO SURRENDER

Mikado orders all his Forces to cease fire

TERMS ACCEPTED – AND NO CONDITIONS

Daily Express, Wednesday, August 15, 1945.

Daily Express, August 15, 1945